SCENIC ROUTES AND COASTAL DRIVES OF NEW BRUNSWICK

A curated guide to towns, festivals, heritage and nature

Marianne and H. A. Eiselt

Formac Publishing Company Limited
Halifax

Formac Publishing Company Limited recognizes the support of the Province of Nova Scotia through Film and Creative Industries Nova Scotia. We are pleased to work in partnership with the Province of Nova Scotia to develop and promote our creative industries for the benefit of all Nova Scotians. We acknowledge the support of the Canada Council for the Arts, which last year invested $157 million to bring the arts to Canadians throughout the country.

Canada Council for the Arts
Conseil des arts du Canada

Cover design: Tyler Cleroux
Cover images: Marianne and H. A. Eiselt

Library and Archives Canada Cataloguing in Publication
Title: Scenic routes and coastal drives of New Brunswick : a curated guide to towns, festivals, heritage and nature / H.A. Eiselt and Marianne Eiselt.
Other titles: Discovering New Brunswick
Names: Eiselt, Marianne, author. | Eiselt, Horst A., 1950- author.
Description: Second edition. | Previously published under title: Discovering New Brunswick. | Includes index.
Identifiers: Canadiana 20220143064 | ISBN 9781459506961 (softcover)
Subjects: LCSH: New Brunswick—Guidebooks. | LCSH: New Brunswick—Description and travel. | LCGFT: Guidebooks.
Classification: LCC FC2457 .E56 2022 | DDC 917.15/1045—dc23

Formac Publishing Company Limited
5502 Atlantic Street
Halifax, Nova Scotia, Canada
B3H 1G4
www.formac.ca

Printed and bound in Canada.

CONTENTS

MAP OF LOCATIONS

INTRODUCTION

It has been twenty years since the first edition of *Discovering New Brunswick* was published, and much has changed since then. We find a new outdoor pioneer village in Saint-François in New Brunswick's Panhandle and learn the story of the fifteen-year-old who started what turned into the chicken capital of the world. We walk through the streets of Sussex, the town that celebrates its past through a colourful outside art gallery, and learn about Canada's oldest cavalry at the town's historic train station. We discover new "old" buildings and facilities at the Village Historique Acadien: an old Irving service station, a cobbler's shop and a cooperage from the early to mid-twentieth century. While visiting Lamèque Island and its beautiful folk art "candy" church, we come upon the Magical Sculpture Trail and its funny wooden statues. There are newly erected heritage places to remember the arrival of Irish and Scottish settlers near Miramichi, such as Wilson's Point. We watch the incoming bore at high tide at Moncton's renewed Bore Park and walk along its path to a monument parklet, signalling where eight German families landed in 1766. We get on a boat from the visitor centre to Beaubears Island where thousands of Acadian refugees perished at Camp d'Espérance in the winter of 1755. We walk along the river on the historical Shiktehawk Trail in Florenceville-Bristol, the site of a battle between the Mi'kmaq and Wolastoqiyik. We have homemade lunch at the humongous Noah's Ark complex near Florenceville-Bristol and stroll in the first class Kingsbrae Garden in St. Andrews.

New natural sites have also been

developed, such as the Fundy Trail Parkway along the Bay of Fundy, featuring seascapes, beaches, a suspension bridge, the Grand Canyon of New Brunswick and many vista points. The Hopewell Rocks Park has received a face lift. It is always exciting to walk around the base of the flowerpot islands on the ocean floor at low tide and return to the site six hours later at high tide.

Unfortunately, a few sites did not survive: the Antique Automobile Museum in Edmundston, Kedgwick's Lumber Camp Museum and the Partridge Island Quarantine Station National Historic Site at the mouth of Saint John Harbour that played a significant role during early immigration to Canada.

This book is an illustrated journey through the province's heritage and natural history, its museums, galleries and craft shops, cathedrals, courthouses, jails and natural gems.

Readers will find familiar sites and favourite festivals in these pages; they will also find new destinations, events and beautiful nature. We hope this book is an invitation to explore all corners of New Brunswick.

1 UPPER RIVER VALLEY

RIVER VALLEY SCENIC DRIVE

The River Valley Scenic Drive from Quebec first traverses the Appalachian mountain range and then follows the mighty Saint John River to Grand Falls. It offers a 677-kilometre (420-mile) stretch of water and some surprising pieces of scenery, history and culture. The first surprise comes upon entering New Brunswick via Quebec's Highway 85 (the Trans-Canada route). Home to 40,000 inhabitants, this region was once called the Republic of Madawaska, a name derived from the language of the early Wolastoqiyik inhabitants, meaning "land of the porcupine." After the Treaty of Paris in

1783, the Madawaska region found itself in the middle of an international boundary dispute between Maine, Quebec and New Brunswick. While awaiting the boundary decision, the region had to be administered, the land parcelled out and forests explored, and so it became a republic unto itself. The Madawaska area includes the city of Edmundston and the Panhandle in north-western New Brunswick, a stone's throw away from the United States of America.

TOP: A water feature at the New Brunswick Botanical Garden.

RIGHT: A wood carving by the artist-in-residence at the garden.

1 SAINT-JACQUES

Arts and Culture

- New Brunswick Botanical Garden

In Saint-Jacques, a parish of Edmundston along the Madawaska River, you can take a stroll in the New Brunswick Botanical Garden, a park of natural beauty. Spread out over 8 hectares (20 acres), more than 70,000 plants are presented in several gardens and two arboretums. Small pathways lead through the rose garden, the shade garden and the alpine garden, which is planted on the ledges of a beautiful waterfall. Don't miss the odd-looking chicken coop with live chickens, and visit the park's artists in residence, who produce and show their crafts here in the summer. A small insectarium in the main building shows camouflaged stick and leaf insects such as the "walking stick." Outside, the garden is indeed an oasis of colour, perfumes and music: Mozart among the roses, Handel in the rhododendrons.

Museums and Historical Sites · Arts and Culture · Parks

TOP: A view of the Bernard-Valcourt Pedestrian Bridge across the Madawaska River.

INSET: The Cathedral of the Immaculate Conception.

Museums and Historical Sites

- Blockhouse at Little Falls (Fortin du Petit-Sault)
- Cathedral of the Immaculate Conception

Parks

- Petit-Sault Park
- Le Prospecteur trails

Edmundston, which is east of the confluence of the mighty Saint John River and the Madawaska River, is the largest city in northeastern New Brunswick. Archibald Fraser started a family pulp mill here in the 1880s. In 1918, he diversified wood harvesting into pulp manufacturing, which remains the mainstay of the city. There is a beautiful viewpoint across the city at the Blockhouse at Little Falls (Fortin du Petit-Sault). This replica blockhouse is worth visiting. The British built the original in 1841 as a line of defense following unresolved land claim issues between them, the Americans and Quebecers. The elegant Bernard-Valcourt pedestrian bridge across the Madawaska River allows panoramic views from the Petit-Sault Park. Picnic tables, benches, statues, plaques and a playground invite you to enjoy this green area at the famous bridge. Across the Madawaska River on the hill, you'll spot the steeples of the impressive Cathedral of the Immaculate Conception. The church honours priest Mgr. W. J. Conway, who was an orphan in Saint-Basile and became an influential educator, church project planner and priest. A large statue of Mgr. Conway stands in a small flower garden in front of the church. Inside the church are beautiful stained windows and a lighted cross behind the altar.

The city of Edmundston also developed a network of trails called Le Prospecteur on the Côte à Blanchette mountain's western slopes. Here the area's well-known miner Bob Leboeuf searched for gold. A trail guide for walking/snowshoeing, supplied at the entrance, outlines the levels of difficulty. If pressed for time, a short, ten-minute walk will lead you to a "belle-vue" lookout across the Madawaska River.

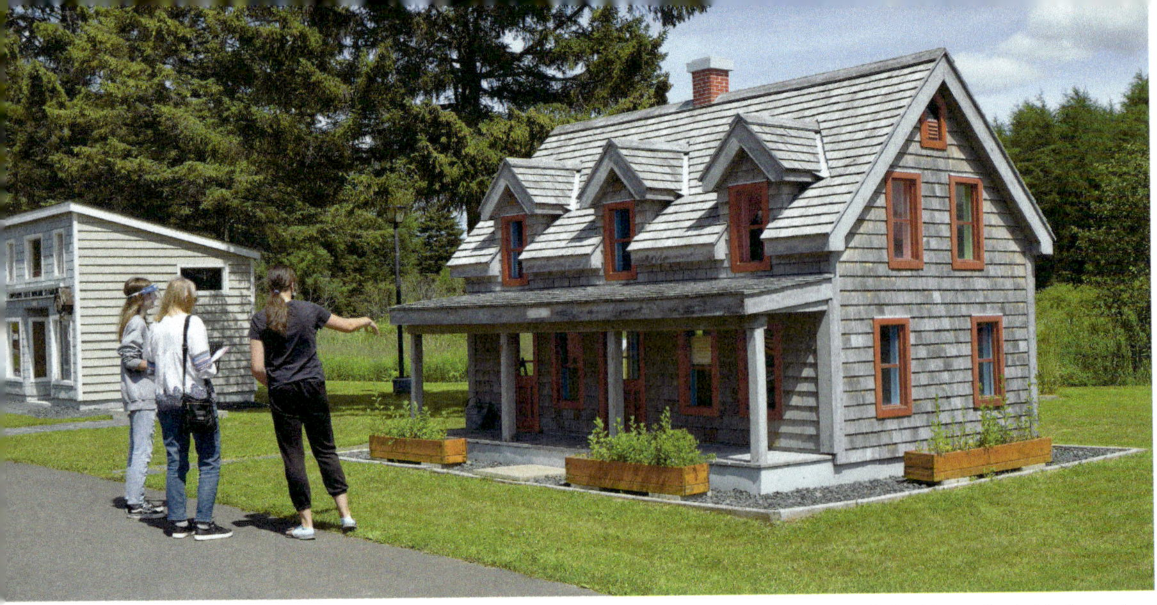

Historical reconstruction at Ledges . . . Pioneers Place near Saint-François de Madawaska.

③ SAINT-FRANÇOIS DE MADAWASKA

Museums and Historical Sites

- Ledges . . . Pioneers Place

The Madawaska-area towns of Clair and Saint-François (formerly Ledges) pay tribute to their pioneering days with the unique outdoor museum, Ledges . . . Pioneers Place, and the historical site in Clair. The museum opened on August 10, 2014, during the Acadian World Congress, following a year-and-a-half-long community effort to plan and build it. The impressive result includes numerous scaled-down reconstructions of private houses, the post office, the red church, the sugar house, Nadeau's first chicken farm, a bread oven, the first slaughterhouse and the regional school of 1930.

The Nadeau family's fifteen-year-old son Louis-Philippe was very entrepreneurial. Early in the 1940s he bought hundreds of chicks and rented other people's abandoned barns to raise them in. In 1945 Louis-Philippe built a small-scale henhouse behind the family residence. Ten years later he built his first large-scale henhouse, adding thirteen more in 1965. These days, the Nadeau family and other chicken producers own more than one hundred henhouses in town. Saint-François proudly calls itself the chicken capital of the world, and features the plump sculpture of a chicken displayed along the road — all from a young man's idea and realization of his dream.

While in town, visit the blacksmith shop of the former Jos. Michaud. The majority of the population in this northwest corner of New Brunswick and into Maine is of Quebec origin. They are known as Brayons, which refers to breaking the flax for spinning.

Museums and Historical Sites   Arts and Culture   Parks

Watching the deluge at Grand Falls.

④ GRAND FALLS  

Museums and Historical Sites

- Grand Falls Museum

Parks

- Grand Falls

Motoring along the Trans-Canada Highway brings you to Grand Falls, where the Saint John River turns into a thunderous waterfall and plummets down a rock-sided ravine. Here the water drops some 23 metres (76 feet) to the bottom of the deep gorge. The wooden stairway down to the wells in the rocks allows a closer look at these large, circular depressions in the rocks, created by the erosive action of swirling water. During the spring thaw, 6 million litres (1.3 million gallons) of water plunges down the falls every second. That's 90 per cent of the volume of Niagara Falls. A short walk towards the dam on Lover's Lane leads to great viewpoints to the top of the rushing waterfall. An iron ring along the way is a reminder of Evangeliste van Morrell, who, in 1904, walked across these falls on an iron cable. Photos of this daredevil act are included in an exhibit at the Grand Falls Museum. Nowadays, a zip line across the spectacular falls area is a safe and fun adventure.

⑤ FLORENCEVILLE-BRISTOL

Museums and Historical Sites

- Potato World

Arts and Culture

- Andrew and Laura McCain Art Gallery

Parks

- Shiktehawk Trail

From the high rolling hill country around Grand Falls, Florenceville-Bristol down to Hartland is the potato farmer's kingdom. Vast potato fields stretch over miles and miles along the Saint John River valley. Potato World, a museum and restaurant in Florenceville-Bristol, pays homage to the pioneer potato farmers and to industrious brothers Harrison and Wallace McCain, who built the McCain Foods empire here. They developed the french fry market for over forty-five years — one third of the frozen french fries eaten in the world come from the McCain company. The museum depicts the beginning of potato farming and processing, so crucial for the survival of early settlers. Educational videos present a variety of topics around the potato. They show the journey of the potato from its origin in Peru to Europe and on to North America, its nutritional value and recent scientific methods used to locate the best land for maximum yield. Florenceville-Bristol also houses the Andrew and Laura McCain Art Gallery, with changing and permanent exhibits of local and international artists. The *Enclave of Cardinals* and the special *One Kilometer of Florenceville* are remarkable ink-on-paper drawings by local artist Colin Smith. The town shows its artistic side through several statues, like the huge tree sculpture by Joe Palmer and the tall *Marich Pole* by Stephen Hutchings depicting cups, houses, a horse and more items to discover.

The town also developed a popular 4-kilometre (2.5-mile) return trail called Shiktehawk. The walking trail meanders along the fast-flowing Shiktehawk river though wooded areas and across small bridges. The name Shiktehawk reportedly comes from a conflict in the area between the Wolastoqiyik and Mi'kmaq. The Chief of the winning Wolastoqiyik called the river Shiktehawk, which means "where he killed him."

Before you leave Florenceville-Bristol, enjoy an espresso at the modern On the Boardwalk: Café & Wine on the main road.

OPPOSITE PAGE: A view of potato fields in the Saint John River valley.

ABOVE: Resting by the river along Shiktehawk Trail.

RIGHT: A tractor on display at the Potato World.

Noah's Ark affordable housing "ship."

6 OAKLAND

Arts and Culture

- Noah's Ark

Continuing south on NB-130 for a few minutes to Burnham Road in Oakland, you'll see a huge building in the form of a ship. This is Noah's Ark, a building like no other. In the 1990s, billionaire Wallace McCain gave Pastor Paul Smith a gift to build small houses and a motel for his bible school. Smith had an idea to build a boat around the existing dormitories, which he completed in the 2010s. Standing 91 metres (300 feet) long, 9 metres (30 feet) wide and 14 metres (45 feet) high, Noah's Ark is a huge, affordable housing "ship." Outside, some chickens roam freely. You can buy their eggs in Noah's Ark Café, where breakfast, soup and baked goods are also sold. This amazing place was not designed for tourists, but tourists are welcome to look around and visit the café, which is open until 2 p.m.

Crossing the Hartland Covered Bridge, the longest covered bridge in the world.

7 HARTLAND

Museums and Historical Sites

- Hartland Covered Bridge

Arts and Culture

- Covered Bridge Potato Chips

Amidst the pastoral beauty, nestled along the Saint John River, lies the town of Hartland. It is home to the longest covered bridge in the world. The Hartland Covered Bridge, a national historic site since 1980, is 391 metres (1,282 feet) long. It was originally built without a roof by a private company in 1901. Being a private venture, there was a toll: Each pedestrian was charged 3 cents, a wagon with a single horse cost 6 cents, and a double team was charged 12 cents. The government bought the bridge in 1906, and in 1920, when ice floes caused severe damage, major repair work was necessary and the roof was added to preserve the wood as much as possible.

Legend has it that every young man in the horse-and-buggy days felt it his right to let his horse rest under a covered bridge while he stole a kiss from the girl beside him. To this day covered bridges are called "kissing bridges." At last count, there were only fifty-eight covered bridges in New Brunswick, and every year more fall victim to decay, accident and vandalism. The magnificent Hartland Bridge remains the finest example of a gradually disappearing tradition.

Still in potato country, a factory tour of the Covered Bridge Potato Chips company in Hartland details modern potato chip production. Heber Hatfield, the mayor of Hartland, started making Hatfield Potato Chips back in the 1940s. Decades later, his son Richard Hatfield came home to help his brother as vice-president of sales of the company, before he also went into politics and eventually became the premier of New Brunswick from 1970 to 1987. The business was sold to Humpty Dumpty Foods in the 1960s. A self-guided tour of the Covered Bridge Potato Chips company explains at different workstations how regular chips and kettle potato chips are cooked by simulating the old-fashioned style of racking them by hand, how quality control is achieved, what filling the bags is all about and more. At the end of the tour, visitors receive a bag of kettle potato chips to taste with a variety of flavours.

8 WOODSTOCK

Museums and Historical Sites

- Woodstock heritage properties

Arts and Culture

- Old Home Week

Parks

- Maliseet Trail
- Hays Falls

From Hartland, the drive south along the Saint John River valley leads to the town of Woodstock. The town celebrates rural life in New Brunswick with its annual Old Home Week in August, featuring a parade, tractor pulls, agricultural displays and tasty treats. Woodstock's heritage is also alive in its fine nineteenth-century architecture. A walking tour around downtown gives a glimpse of former times.

At 128 Connell is the classical revival mansion built in 1839 and owned by the honourable Charles Connell, who was a successful politician and postmaster until he took the incredible step of issuing an official five-cent stamp in his own image. This misguided ego trip caused such a commotion that he was forced to resign from public office. The Carleton County Historical Society owns the property and operates it as a museum. On the upper floor is a room with unusual instruments and also a display depicting the work of Tappan Adney (1868–1950), who lived among the Wolastoqiyik people to learn about their language and boat-building skills. He was a travel writer, journalist, artist and naturalist. Among his best-known literary feats is

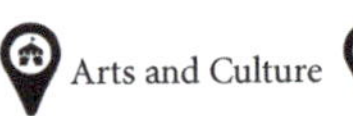

his account of the gold rush to the Yukon in 1897, which he covered for *Harper's Weekly*. Academics at Harvard and other institutions often sought Adney's advice on the folklore and languages of Indigenous peoples.

At 119 Chapel stands the Judge Jones House with its steeply pitched gables and unusual, pointed Gothic windows over the entrance. This green and white house is a rare example of picturesque architecture with Gothic features. At 100 St. John Street stands the impressive house of the pharmacist Paxton Baird. Built in 1898, the mansion features high Victorian styles with an Italianate hipped roof and bays and Greek revival pediments. The Bairds sold it to the apothecary E. W. Mair in 1910.

At 129 Chapel stands the Women's Institute Home, built in 1910 for merchant Alex Benn. In 1953 it became a home for aged members of the Women's Institute. Funding for the purchase came in part from the proceeds of selling 20,000 copies of the *Victoria Women's Institute Cookbook*. This home became the first of its type in Canada. A self-guided heritage walking tour of historic buildings is available from the Carleton County Historical Society.

Just south of Woodstock on Route 165 is the trailhead of the Maliseet Trail, traditionally a portage route. The easy to moderate, one-hour return hiking trail leads down to the beautiful, cascading Hays Falls with a picnic table.

OPPOSITE PAGE: Charles Connell House and Carleton County Historical Society museum, built in 1839.

INSET: Tin soldiers on display inside Charles Connell House.

BELOW: Baird-Mair House, built in 1898.

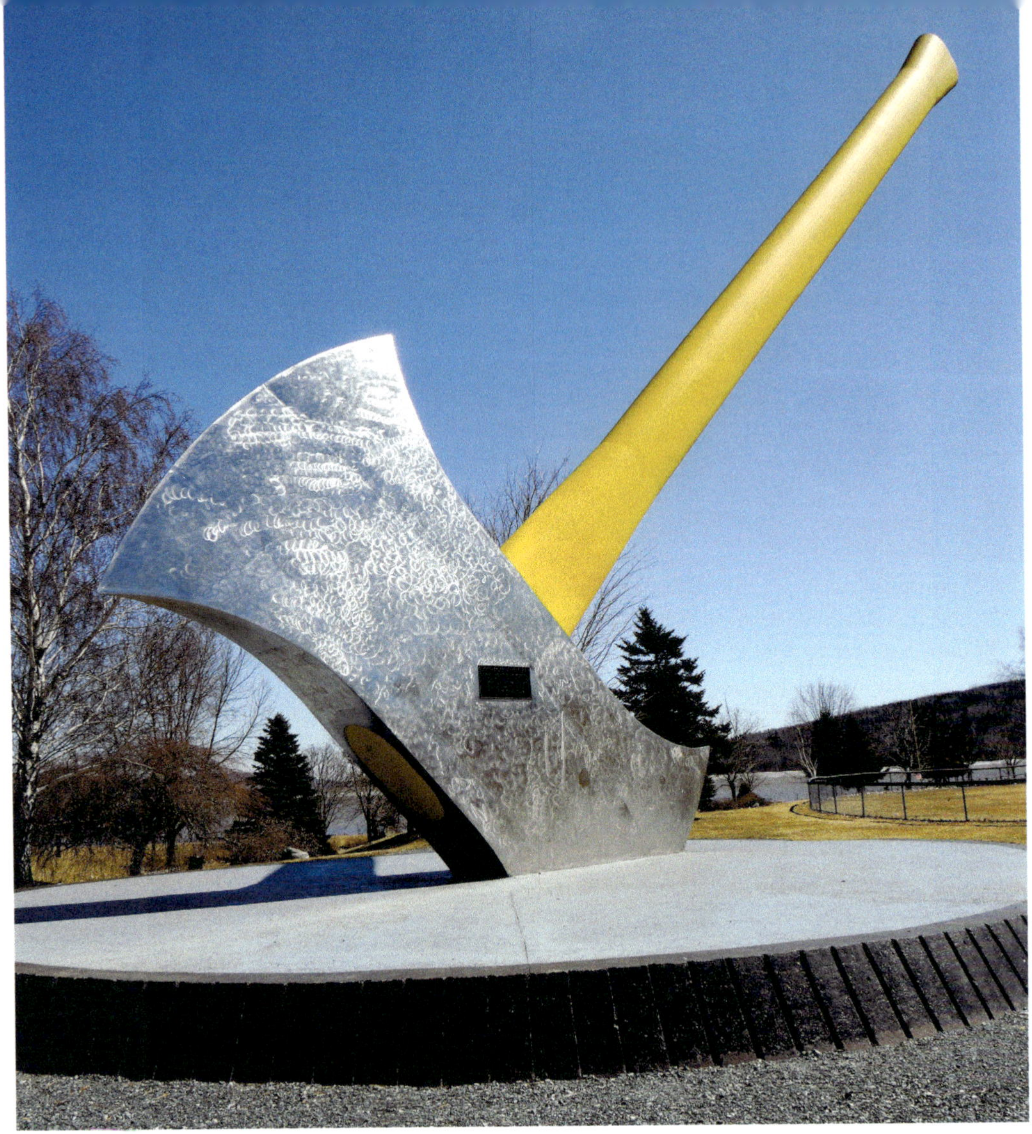

A view of the world's largest axe.

Arts and Culture

- World's largest axe

Further down the Saint John River valley, the small town of Nackawic is home of the world's largest axe, an almost 20-metre (65-foot) tall, double-sided axe with a stainless-steel blade. This impressive statue at a park at the river's banks stands for the lumbering tradition of the area and commemorates the selection of Nackawic as the Forest Capital of Canada.

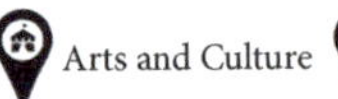

2 LOWER RIVER VALLEY

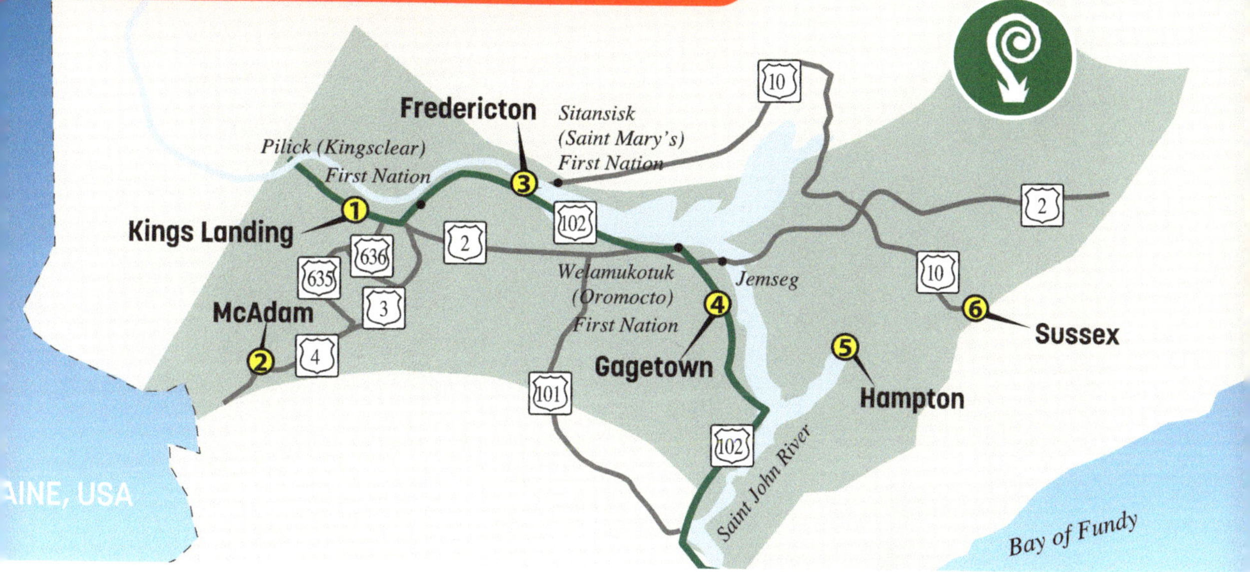

Fredericton
Sitansisk (Saint Mary's) First Nation
Pilick (Kingsclear) First Nation
Kings Landing
McAdam
Welamukotuk (Oromocto) First Nation
Jemseg
Gagetown
Hampton
Sussex
Saint John River
Bay of Fundy
MAINE, USA

① KINGS LANDING

Museums and Historical Sites

- Kings Landing Historical Settlement

Kings Landing Historical Settlement, just off the Trans-Canada Highway 37 kilometres (23 miles) west of Fredericton on the banks of the Saint John River, is a re-creation of a nineteenth-century New Brunswick village. When the nearby Mactaquac Dam was constructed in 1963, a number of houses that otherwise would have been submerged in the head pond were transported to this site. Now about seventy buildings, the active lumber and grist mills and the farms with pigs, sheep, bulls and horses form a living museum on a 121-hectare (300-acre) site. Different from other historical, open-air museums that

A demonstration of broom making.

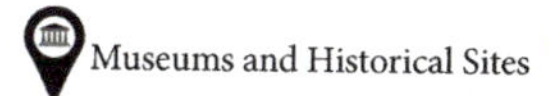

Museums and Historical Sites · Arts and Culture · Parks

portray a specific decade, Kings Landing's history spans predominantly from the late eighteenth century to the Victorian era. The settlers along the Saint John River are American Loyalists and their descendants, followed later by immigrants from the British Isles and Ireland. The life of the Wolastoqiyik, the original inhabitants of this river valley, is also depicted on site with exhibitions of a canoe, birch bark baskets and moccasins.

The costumed guides take on the role of their houses' owners and visitors can hop on horse-and-wagon rides and instantly feel immersed in these bygone times. Mostly on weekends, musicians play traditional music and perform short plays in the Theatre Barn. The fall auction, maple syrup making and the scarecrow competition are other popular activities.

The Loyalists were former residents of Britain's thirteen American colonies who fought for the British Crown under

TOP: Taking a wagon ride at Kings Landing.

INSET: Sap boiling to make maple syrup.

The Kings Landing sawmill, still working with 1830s technology.

George III against George Washington and the creation of the United States. At the end of the American War of Independence (1775–1783), the loyal colonists, who had supported the losing side, went into exile. In 1783 a group of approximately 15,000 Loyalists arrived mostly from New York City to settle along the Saint John River valley as far north as Woodstock. These settlers founded both Saint John and Fredericton. The Loyalists were entitled to free land grants and other government help during their first three years in New Brunswick. With back-breaking labour, they cleared the forested lands along the Saint John River for farming. Those who survived the harsh weather, in tents and drafty shelters, can be accurately described as the founders of New Brunswick: Its creation from what used to be Nova Scotia in 1784 was largely the result of the petitions of Loyalist residents who did not want their affairs run from Halifax. Furthermore, the Loyalists introduced an independent legal system to New Brunswick.

Several Kings Landing buildings are among those built by first-generation Loyalists or their children. A saltbox-style house, originally located on Westmorland Street in Fredericton, is one of the earliest houses on the site. This small dwelling was the childhood home of Loyalist Peter Fisher, who became a successful merchant and prominent New Brunswick author of the 1825 *Sketches of New Brunswick*.

The restored Hagerman House, built in 1830.

Another very old structure is an octagonal privy built in the 1790s for the large Loyalist country estate of Chief Justice John Saunders. This fancy, noble outhouse, now located in the Ingraham dwelling complex, is a fitting memorial to Loyalist pretensions to grandeur.

The Hagerman House, built in the 1830s in the popular neoclassical style of that time, followed a local tradition of framing the house with hand-hewn timbers, post-and-beam style. The house, restored to its 1870 appearance, showcases beautiful furniture made by St. Stephen–based cabinetmaker John Warren Moore. In the elegant Victorian dining room, typically reserved for special occasions, Moore's craftsmanship includes the dining table, the china cabinet and the plant stand. Moore's fine work is also evident in the parlour, with the eye-catching "lady's" and "gentleman's" chairs with their elegant cabriole legs, the large desk and the church-like Gothic glass doors.

Another example of neoclassical symmetry is the home of Ira Ingraham, a New Brunswick–born son of Loyalist parents. His father had joined the American Regiment at the outset of the war, before leaving to settle along the Saint John River valley. Ira's sister Hannah gives an account of their initial hardship: "We lived in a tent at St. Anne's until father got a house ready." It was early winter when her father led them into the new house where "no floor" was laid,

A spinning wheel and bed made in the 1800s inside Ingraham House, built in 1840.

"no windows, no chimney, no door, but we had a roof at last . . . a good fire was blazing, and mother had a big loaf of bread." The family's condition improved, and Ira and his brother John established a prosperous farm, tannery and leather working shop. The Ingraham House was built in 1840, where Ira, his wife, Olive, three of their adult sons, a cousin and the unmarried Aunt Hannah, who presided over family life and had a reputation for healing the sick, lived quite comfortably.

In its interior, the Ingraham House showcases the work of New Brunswick's famous furniture maker Thomas Nisbet (1777–1850), who came to New Brunswick from Scotland in 1812 and set up shop in Saint John. Nisbet's high-quality furniture includes the large mahogany desk and four-poster bed, the sofa table and game table as well as the Regency-style sofa. These pieces are evidence of excellence, a reputation which New Brunswick's furniture makers enjoyed in the nineteenth century. The most striking feature of the Ingraham estate is its Victorian flower garden with its profusion of scents and colours from early June to September.

The Jones House is quite different from the other homes, as it is built of stone. According to family legend, Thomas Jones was in the midst of building his house when he heard that his wife had just given birth to their first son. But Jones, perhaps concerned that his wife and newborn son would soon want to move in to the new house, continued laying stone and putting

ABOVE: Killeen Cabin, built in 1825 with square logs.

RIGHT: Hackling flax in Killeen Cabin.

in windows, never pausing to see his new family member. The Jones House, with its solid stone construction and rich interior decorations, reflects the lifestyle of wealthy Loyalist families of the nineteenth century. Thomas Jones was a justice of the peace, captain and paymaster in the militia and an Anglican church warden.

The arrival of new immigrants in the 1830s produced a shift in the population of New Brunswick. The Loyalists, now in their second and third generations, were joined by settlers from the British Isles. The Killeen family was one of many hardy, industrious couples who fled poverty in Ireland, but the land they received was unproductive and thus their farms were marginal, barely feeding the family. The Killeen Cabin, built in 1825 of squared logs, is an example of the first houses built by immigrants. The furnishings are simple and sparse, as there was money only for necessities.

The Saint John River and its tributaries provided the necessary waterpower to operate sawmills and grist mills. Kings Landing sawmill, operational today, offers a look at 1830s technology. Its saw cuts a foot a minute, so it would take about three quarters of an hour to saw a full-sized tree. At the nearby grist mill, dating from 1885, buckwheat is ground into bran and flour.

Other rural industries include the blacksmith shop, carpenter shop and printing office. The cooper was also important because he supplied barrels and casks used as shipping and storage containers of the pre-industrial era. Larger industries such as carriage and sleigh factories and sash and door factories were developed by mid-century.

ABOVE: A demonstration by a re-enactor in the blacksmith's shop.

BELOW: Auction at Kings Landing.

ABOVE: St. Mark's Church.

LEFT: Riverside Presbyterian Church.

The C. B. Ross Sash & Door Factory, seen in replica at Kings Landing, displays the equipment used in building doors and windows in early industrial society.

The Parish School at Kings Landing, dating back to 1840, is a small building with simple desks and benches. The blackboard is literally made of wooden boards blackened with shellac and stove blacking. The Bible was the major book used by the schoolteachers, perhaps with additional books supplied by the pupils' parents. Students learned by memorization and repetition, and schoolwork competed for time with farm and household work.

The government also provided for the Church of England congregations, but not to other denominations. Most of the Loyalist Tory elite were followers of the Church of England. However, many New Brunswickers joined Baptist movements, which became popular in the early nineteenth century. By mid-century, the Church of England had begun a revival under Bishop John Medley. St. Mark's Church in Kings Landing can trace back its origin to Medley's influence.

The King's Head Inn, an example of classical revival style, is representative of a Saint John River valley inn of 1855. Inns were

ABOVE: The King's Head Inn, still serving guests!

RIGHT: Performing for guests at the King's Head Inn.

essential in the nineteenth century, when travel by road or river was a slow affair. Inns were commonly called "halfway houses," referring to breaking the journey at mid-point between home and destination. Taverns had to provide at least two beds to qualify for the governmental liquor license. Beds were sometimes scarce, but food and drink were abundant: "Everything to satisfy a hungry man is here. Ham and eggs, fowl, venison of moose or deer (found within a hundred yards), pies, doughnuts, and the inevitable applesauce," wrote W. T. Baird in *Seventy Years of New Brunswick Life*. Today, the dining room of King's Head Inn serves meals from authentic Victorian recipes, and refreshments that can be enjoyed in the adjoining green area. The taproom serves tasty ale. The bakery at the Axe and Plough Café sells delicious homemade bread, brownies and muffins — bring some home along with memories of your visit to Kings Landing.

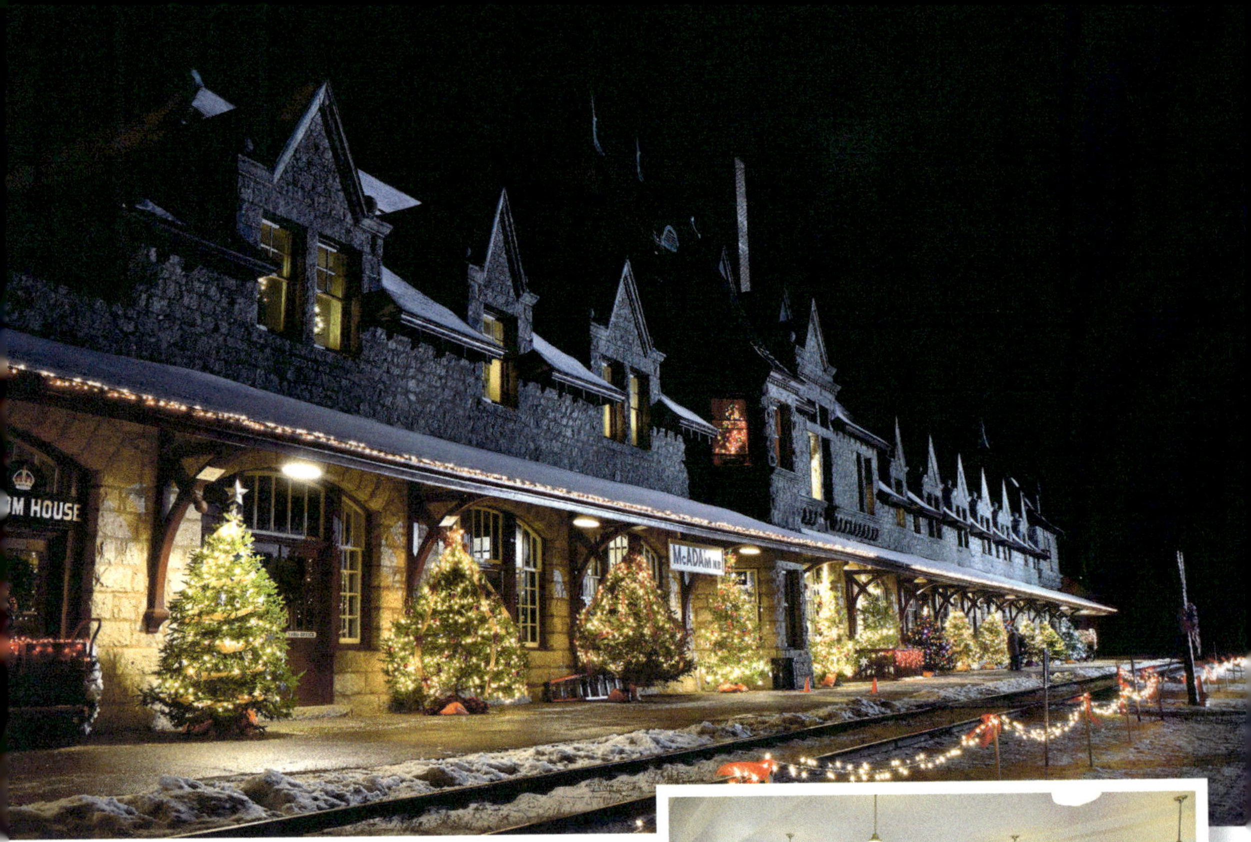

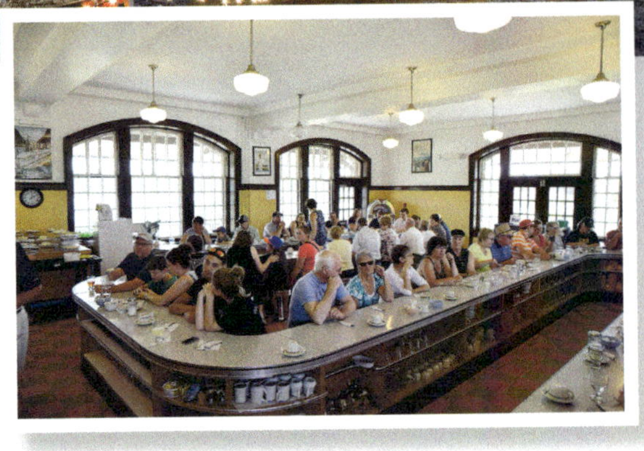

② McADAM

Museums and Historical Sites

- Historic Railway Station

The chateau-like railway station cum hotel in the town of McAdam, built in 1900, was the only Canadian Pacific Railway line into Atlantic Canada. Many immigrant trains bound for Ontario and the Prairies passed through McAdam. In 1994 Via Rail's Atlantic passenger train was abandoned. After many years of fundraising and restoration, this national and provincial historic site opened as a museum and visitor centre. Captivating guided tours are offered throughout the summer months. In December, Christmas at the Station features amazingly beautiful, decorated rooms throughout the main floor, and lighted Christmas trees inside and out are certain to get you in the season's spirit.

TOP: Christmas at the railway station, built in 1900.

INSET: Eating in the 1960s diner.

Christ Church Cathedral, built 1845-1853.

③ FREDERICTON

Museums and Historical Sites

- Christ Church Cathedral
- Officers' Quarters
- Soldiers' Stone Barracks
- Guard House
- Militia Arms Store
- City hall
- School Days Museum
- Fredericton Region Museum
- Legislative Assembly Building

Arts and Culture

- Boyce Farmers Market
- Beaverbrook Art Gallery
- Christ Church Summer Recital Series
- Harvest Music Festival
- Shakespeare in the Park
- Highland Games

Parks

- The Green River Walk
- Bill Thorpe Walking Bridge

Fredericton, the City of Stately Elms, was built alongside the Saint John River. This transportation lifeline brought settlers to these fertile shores, and because of its distance from the ocean, was chosen by Governor Carleton in 1785 as the provincial capital. The town was named in honour of Prince Frederick, second son of George III. The governor and his Loyalist supporters envisioned "a haven for the King's friends" — supported by the Church of England — with a university to prepare their sons for careers in government, the military or respectable professions such as law. Land was set aside for a university, a military compound and an Anglican church. King's College was founded in 1785 by the United Empire Loyalists, and in 1859 reorganized into the non-denominational University of New Brunswick.

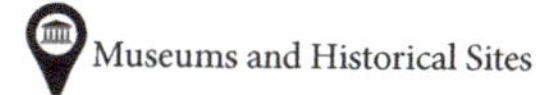
Museums and Historical Sites

Arts and Culture
Parks

ABOVE: Learning about the First World War at the Military History Museum.

BELOW: A re-enactor inside the School Days Museum.

Because of Fredericton's capital status and proximity to the American border, military personnel of the 57th, the 54th and the 104th Foot Regiments were stationed here. Canada's oldest regular infantry regiment, the Royal Canadian Regiment, was raised in "Frederick's Town" on December 21, 1883. Today, the Officers' Quarters, the Soldiers' Stone Barracks, the Guard House and the Militia Arms Store are testimony to the army's importance to Fredericton's early history.

For much of the nineteenth and well into the twentieth century New Brunswick's capital city remained a quiet provincial backwater, its local politicians — many of them descendants of the Loyalists — seemingly more interested in keeping the status quo than in encouraging commercial growth. They learned little from the success of Alexander "Boss" Gibson, who created and

ran Marysville, across the river, where his cotton mill was one of Canada's largest in 1885. Marysville, now a part of Fredericton, has a large brick cotton mill at the banks of the Nashwaak River. Since 1985, the large building has undergone major restoration for office use by the provincial government. The former company town showcases streets lined with rows of bygone brick workers' tenements, managers' ornate homes and stores. What the industrious and well-respected Boss Gibson began as a modest mill operation became a prosperous town. Most of the town's workers were employed at the mill. Instead of driving through this former mill town, visitors may want to walk or bike the groomed trails along the Nashwaak River to the Gibson Pavilion and beyond, where brick houses and remnants of the mill operation still remain to remind us of this bygone era.

During the First and Second World Wars, Fredericton was the site of a basic training centre for the Canadian Armed Forces. In 1958 Camp Gagetown opened in Oromocto, thereby bolstering the local economy. Today, Canadian Forces Base (CFB) Gagetown is Canada's second largest military base — with an 1,100-square-kilometre (684-square-mile) training area — and one of New Brunswick's largest employers. At New Brunswick's Military Museum on the base, visitors learn about New Brunswick's role in military campaigns. Attractive displays inform visitors about the raids among French rivals in the 1640s, the long February march of the 104th (New Brunswick) Regiment to defend Upper Canada against American forces, the Boer War and the Royal Canadian Navy's wireless station near Moncton, which tracked German U-boats in 1944 during the Second World War, and Soviet warships and Cuban nuclear missile ships in 1962 during the Cold War.

Fredericton city hall.

One of Fredericton's main architectural attractions is City Hall. Erected in 1876 at the corner of Queen and York Streets, it is the oldest city hall still in use in the Maritime provinces. In recent years, interior renovations and exterior restoration of the original building have been undertaken to bring it in line with current standards. The old building once included the city office,

Ceremonial guards outside the Guard House.

council chamber, magistrate's office, jail, farmers' market and even an opera house. The tower clock, with its eight-foot dials, copper hands and reliable chimes, has been keeping Frederictonians on time since 1876. The fountain in front of city hall features Fredericton's very own "Freddy, the nude dude," as he is affectionately called. Across from city hall, located at the back entrance of the Justice Building, was the site of the former Provincial Normal School and Teacher's College, now a School Days Museum. It is interesting to see the progression from no formal schooling in Canada to the Provincial Normal School, starting in 1871. The older generation may remember the Dick and Jane picture books (displayed in the museum) for easy reading, used in public schools between 1940 and 1960. At the museum, there is also a fun re-enactment of a lesson in a one-room school to give a feel for this rural schooling that was discontinued in 1968. Learn your algebra before you attend!

One block east of city hall on Queen Street is Officers' Square and the Officers' Quarters, one of the garrison city's remaining historic areas. During the summer, there is an hourly ceremony of the changing of the guard and performances at the outdoor theatre. The Officers' Quarters building facing the Parade Square represents an architectural style typical of the colonial period: stone arches and iron handrails and staircase. Today, the building houses the Fredericton Region Museum featuring

ABOVE: New Brunswick Legislative Building.

LEFT: The spiral staircase inside the Legislative Building.

New Brunswick Indigenous, domestic and military history. Nearby we find Boyce Farmers Market on George Street, which was relocated to this site in 1952. Each Saturday morning, it is a favourite place for Frederictonians to see, be seen and yes, to purchase fresh farm products.

Further east on Queen Street is the majestic provincial Legislative Assembly Building, an impressive sandstone structure in Second Empire style. It has been the seat of government since 1882. A guided tour of this elegant building passes through hallways lined with pictures of former lieutenant-governors, into the legislative chamber. In a cabinet the mace is displayed. The mace — the traditional sign of power — is placed next to the table in the chamber whenever the house is in session. One of the most impressive elements in the beautifully decorated assembly chamber is the throne or Speaker's chair under a canopy bearing the carving of the royal coat of arms. It serves as the throne when the lieutenant-governor enters the chamber, and during the legislative sessions it is the Speaker's chair. The chamber is decorated in late Victorian style. The fancy wallpaper

Gallery 78 in downtown Fredericton, with the tower on the Legislative Building visible in the background.

is Japonesque, the carpet from England is in traditional green and the chandeliers are made of brass with crystal prisms.

The tour continues by climbing part of the 12-metre (40-foot) free-standing (and slightly sloping) spiral staircase. Its fancy woodwork includes walnut, cherry, ash and pine. Upstairs, from the visitors' gallery, there is a view down to the elegant chamber. Back on the main floor is the legislative library, with its treasured volume of 435 hand-coloured copper engravings of John James Audubon's *Birds of America*. The library's holdings also include a 1763 copy of the *Domesday Book*, a land registry dating back to 1086. Across from the Legislative Assembly is the Beaverbrook Art Gallery, a gift from Lord Beaverbrook, the declared "native son of New Brunswick," who was raised in New Brunswick, built a publishing empire and served Britain as minister of aircraft production during the Second World War. The famous gallery houses a prestigious collection of British paintings by Thomas Gainsborough, J. M. W. Turner and John Constable. The impressive, oversized *Santiago el Grande*, by Salvador Dali, is permanently on display in the new wing. The gallery also has an extensive permanent collection of paintings by Cornelius Krieghoff, among them the celebrated *Merrymaking* and the *Cheating at the Tolls*. In the permanent collection are also works of art by the Group of Seven, Emily Carr and David Milne. The gallery also features period furniture, china and a museum café.

Within clear view of the Beaverbrook Art Gallery is Crocket House, another Fredericton landmark. It houses Gallery 78, one of New Brunswick's oldest commercial galleries, representing distinguished Canadian artists and artisans such as Molly Lamb Bobak and Bruno Bobak, Tom Forrestall, Cheryl Bogart, Gordon Dunphy and Mary and Christopher Pratt.

Further along and on the opposite side of "the Green," the local name for the park along the bank of the Saint John River, is

The University of New Brunswick across the Saint John River.

Christ Church Cathedral, a national historic site since 1983. Construction of the massive church began in 1845, modelled after a medieval church in England and built under the strong influence of Bishop John Medley. The natural stone used for its construction was quarried in New Brunswick, and most of the woodwork, such as the wainscot panelling along both sides of the nave, is made of butternut, adding character and atmosphere to this impressive cathedral. Each year, at the Summer Recital Series, Christ Church Cathedral offers free noon hour concerts where local musicians sing or play pieces on the organ, piano, violin, cello and guitar. The short Green River Walk passes under the former railroad bridge and continues past beautiful homes in various architectural styles, such as the stately house at 258 Waterloo Row, now the residence of the president of the University of New Brunswick.

Since its transformation into a footbridge as part of the Trans Canada Trail network in 1997, the CN Railway bridge stretching over the Saint John River is a favourite place for Frederictonians to stroll and enjoy views of the city. From the footbridge, renamed Bill Thorpe Walking Bridge, several walking/biking trails lead through the city, often along the Nashwaak and Saint John Rivers.

Fredericton hosts the annual Harvest Music Festival, which draws visitors from near and far. Musical performances are held throughout venues at the downtown core and some free concerts are run, often in Officers' Square.

Theatrical performances are also popular in the city: there is Shakespeare in the Park, which is held in the summer for several weeks at Fredericton's large Odell Park. Downtown at Officers' Square is another venue for outdoor theatre. Often, these productions are directed by professors and

Playing the bagpipes and throwing kegs at the Scottish Highland Games.

performed by students of the University of New Brunswick.

A special weekend of Scottish cultural entertainment is staged yearly on the grounds of the old Government House, the seat of office for New Brunswick's lieutenant-governor and also a national and provincial historic site. The two-day Highland Games pay tribute to the Maritimes' Scottish ancestry. This cultural event dates back to the fateful Battle of Culloden in 1746, when thousands of Highlanders lost their lives. In order to retain their cultural identity, some Scots joined the British army or emigrated to Canada, mainly to the Maritimes and Upper Canada.

The annual Highland Games feature dancing, piping and drumming competitions, massed bands and heavyweight events, the latter including "putting the weight over the bar," "throwing the hammer" and, most famously, "tossing the caber." The caber is a 7-metre (20-foot), 66-kilogram (150-pound) pole that must be flipped over by the athlete. If the piping, drumming and athletic events leave visitors hungry or thirsty, they can enjoy Scottish fare, such as haggis and Irn-Bru, a typical Scottish soft drink, or the traditional afternoon tea with freshly baked scones and other homemade sweets.

Ferry crossing the Saint John River between Gagetown and Jemseg.

4 GAGETOWN

Museums and Historical Sites

- Tilley House Museum
- Fort Jemseg

Arts and Culture

- Greig Pottery
- Loomcrofters Studio

The lower Saint John River valley is a large watershed dotted with charming peninsulas, islands and quaint villages that are served by small ferries. More than half a dozen ferries operate toll-free for the public across the Saint John River and its tributaries.

One of these ferries across the river operates from Gagetown, a community with a distinctly artistic flavour: Greig Pottery on Front Street is Gagetown's trademark and so are the loomcrofters. Galleries and artisans produce and sell paintings, jewellery, soap, quilts, woven goods, clothing and wood items in this charming town. The main road on the shores of the Saint John River also provides access to the marina, Steamers' Bed & Breakfast with fine dining and Sir Leonard Tilley's boyhood home. Now a museum, this gracious home is where Sir Leonard Tilley, who became one of Canada's Fathers of Confederation, was born on May 18, 1818. A costumed guide welcomes visitors to the thirteen-room house. The Loyalist kitchen features a huge fireplace, built with handmade bricks. Another room in the house served originally as the office

The boyhood home of Sir Leonard Tilley, built in 1786.

of Dr. Stickles, who built this house in 1786, though it looks more like a torture chamber than a doctor's office.

The Gagetown loomcrofters are housed in a small studio built in 1761 as a farm outbuilding. Around 1945, it was moved to the outskirts of town. In December 2014, the historic Loomcrofters Studio was moved again, this time on a flatbed truck next to its destination at the Tilley House. After many repair works, it reopened in 2017. In the showroom, two loomcrofters typically work on placemats, table runners, tartan ties or tartan afghans. This is no mass production — it takes about four days to weave an afghan. The traditional craft of weaving became popular in Gagetown thanks to the late designer, weaver and teacher Patricia Jenkins. In 1940 Jenkins created the official Royal Canadian Air Force tartan, and in the 1950s she designed the official New Brunswick tartan.

When you take the ferry from Gagetown across the Saint John River, the drive is scenic and also of historic significance. Only a short distance from the small ferry terminal, several concrete steps lead up an embankment with a beautiful view on top. This was the place of Fort Jemseg, built as a trading post by English troops in 1659, when they possessed Acadia. A plaque details a few interesting facts about the fort.

ABOVE: Kings County Museum and Gaol.

INSET: An old cell inside the museum.

5 HAMPTON

Museums and Historical Sites

- Kings County Museum and Gaol

Arts and Culture

- Hooper Studios Gallery

Hampton is another beautiful small town in the Lower Saint John River valley. The famous sculptor John Hooper (1926–2006) resided here and produced expressive, multi-coloured wooden statues you can find in Saint John's Market Square, on Parliament Hill in Ottawa, and in Toronto, Vancouver and Los Angeles. Today, the Hooper Studios Gallery offers workshops and restores Hooper's sculptures.

The Kings County Museum and Gaol is an interesting place that you enter through an indoor covered bridge! On a tour, you see and hear the story of a unique quilt, made from Confederation ladies' dresses by Hampton resident Fannie Parlee in 1864. Recently restored and under glass, this huge quilt with numerous different border stitches is a remarkable historic specimen. Also notable nearby is the snowball quilt — made by an eleven-year-old girl! The gaol (jail) next door was moved here from Kingston in 1871. Over its 100 years of use it has seen some manipulating scoundrels, like Henry More Smith. Hear about his crime, his fortune telling and puppet shows in jail and his ingenious escapes. The jail has been closed since 1971, but the stories live on.

6 SUSSEX

Museums and Historical Sites

- 8th Hussars Museum
- Agricultural Museum

Arts and Culture

- Atlantic Balloon Fiesta
- Sussex murals
- Sussex Car Show
- Harvest Day

Parks

- Sussex Bluff Trail
- Dutch Valley farms

TOP: A view across Dutch Valley from the Sussex Bluff Trail.

BELOW: Balloons in the air at the Atlantic Balloon Fiesta.

When you drive through Sussex, you cannot miss the colourful murals around each corner. These outdoor paintings on buildings depict historical scenes of life in Sussex, such as the beautiful Italianate decor of the Exhibition Building of 1861, early pioneer settlers, royal visits in 1939, 1985 and 2002, maple syrup harvesting, the merchants of Sussex and education for Loyalist and Mi'kmaw children, to name a few. An official mural walking guide is available at the 8th Hussars Museum.

Sussex was also home to Canada's oldest Cavalry Regiment, dating back to 1848, when the hussars were actually part-time farm workers and part-time militia. These soldiers brought their own horses to train at Camp Sussex. In the 1930s, tanks and motorized vehicles made horses obsolete, but the hussar spirit remained. You can learn more about the 8th Hussars in a nice museum, located in the historic train station, and you will be surprised about their active worldwide service.

Sussex is also home to the annual Atlantic Balloon Fiesta. Back in 1986, several prominent local business people wanted to attract visitors to Sussex in the off-season. They invited some maritime balloonists to Sussex for a fall weekend and the fiesta was born. It now includes a craft show and an antique car show held on the weekend after Labour Day. Nearby, the Agricultural Museum of New Brunswick in Sussex comes to life during Harvest Day at the end of September with wagon rides, demonstrations of antique farm equipment, grain-thrashing and butter making, an auction and a BBQ.

Sussex is the dairy centre of New Brunswick and has produced quality milk, cream, butter, ice cream and cheese for over 100 years. Adjoining Sussex is the village of Sussex Corner with its green pastures and Dutch Valley dairy farms. Dutch Valley is best seen from the popular Sussex Bluff Trail, a 5-kilometre (3-mile) return trail with amazing vistas.

3 WESTERN FUNDY COAST

MAINE, USA
Saint John River
Peskotomuhkati at Skutik (Passamaquoddy) First Nation
Bayside
Saint John
Saint Croix Island
Ministers Island
St. Andrews
Bay of Fundy
Herring Cove Provincial Park
Campobello Island
Grand Manan Island

FUNDY COASTAL DRIVE

The 450-kilometre (281-mile) Fundy Coastal Drive offers a variety of incredible natural phenomena. The Bay of Fundy, that remarkable body of tidal water, has shaped New Brunswick's southern shoreline. There is nothing like it in the marine world. Its full-moon tides can reach 8.5 metres (28 feet). Its many whirlpools and swirling currents act as giant pumps bringing in a mixture of tiny marine organisms that in turn lure all kinds of creatures: from schools of herring and mackerel to bluefin tuna to minke, humpback or right whales.

These marine riches first drew humans to the Bay of Fundy's shores. Indigenous peoples harvested clam beds and caught herring and salmon in weirs. The first European settlement attempt took place over the winter of 1604–5 when an ill-fated expedition led by Samuel de Champlain encamped on the tiny Saint Croix Island, now an international historic site, operated by Canada and the United States.

① BAYSIDE

Museums and Historical Sites

- Saint Croix Island Exhibit

An outdoor exhibit operated by Parks Canada, located at Bayside, New Brunswick, across from the island, shows the hardship the expedition members had to endure during an unusually severe winter and a scurvy epidemic. The Saint Croix Island International Historic Site can also be visited near Calais, Maine.

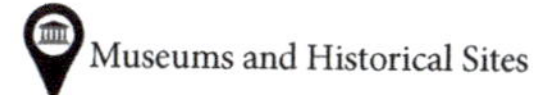

Museums and Historical Sites

Arts and Culture

Parks

The famous Algonquin Resort, built in 1902.

2 ST. ANDREWS

Museums and Historical Sites

- Ministers Island Historic Site
- Sheriff Andrews House
- Ross Memorial Museum
- Charlotte County Court House and Gaol
- St. Andrews Blockhouse

Arts and Culture

- Algonquin Resort
- Water Street and Wharf
- Huntsman Marine Science Centre

Parks

- Kingsbrae Garden

Along the Fundy Coastal Drive lies the town of St. Andrews by-the-Sea, one of the country's most beautiful seaside resorts. Once a haven for United Empire Loyalists fleeing the American Revolution in 1783, St. Andrews remains steeped in traditional charm and luxurious accommodations.

Boasting "no hay fever and a railway" in the late nineteenth century, gracious hotels were built to make St. Andrews the first choice in Canadian resorts. The Algonquin, New Brunswick's most famous resort hotel and a town landmark, was built by local businessmen. In 1902, Sir William Van Horne and Sir Thomas Shaughnessy, two American-born industrialists who rose to fame and fortune in Montreal as heads of the Canadian Pacific Railway Company, bought the stylish Tudor revival hotel and created a booming tourist town. Van Horne also purchased Ministers Island from the Loyalist reverend Samuel Andrews, now a provincial and federal historic site accessible from St. Andrews at low tide. He built a grand summer residence, a circular bath house and tidal swimming pool and an impressive barn for his prized Dutch cattle. Shaughnessy and Van Horne had international connections

Museums and Historical Sites · Arts and Culture · Parks

that were soon reflected in the Algonquin's clientele. The business and social elite of Boston, New York and Montreal helped establish the hotel and the town. Today, the Algonquin Resort is a castle by the sea that features exquisite accommodations, fine dining and a wealth of recreational facilities — including the signature eighteen-hole ocean view golf course.

The town's core has been designated a national historic district and several homes — some over 200 years old — have been marked with descriptive plaques. St. Andrews's streets follow the traditional grid pattern, with street names such as King, Queen, Elizabeth, William and Princess Royal, signifying the town's Loyalist heritage.

The heart of downtown is Water Street. As the name suggests, it runs parallel to the shore. Water Street is lined with craft shops, galleries, boutiques, coffee shops, café, fine restaurants, quaint inns and the town wharf. All the downtown stores were designed to fit in with the architectural heritage — among them a gas station, a garage and a supermarket.

ABOVE: Visitors enjoying the shops on Water Street.

INSET: The kitchen in Sheriff Andrews House, built in 1820.

Just a few steps off Water Street on King is Sheriff Andrews House, built in

ABOVE: Visiting Ross Memorial House, built in 1824.

LEFT: Owner's bedroom in Ross Memorial House.

1820 by Elisha Shelton Andrews, sheriff of Charlotte County and son of Reverend Samuel Andrews. Nine period-furnished rooms with working fireplaces tell of middle-class domestic life in a seaport town in the early nineteenth century. Sheriff Andrews had seven children and two servants; the latter lived in the servants' quarters on the third floor, reached by a separate staircase. A drawing room on the ground floor contains a strongbox, undoubtedly for the sheriff's documents. Three leather fire buckets hang on pegs in the hallway, as required by law. In the basement is a large kitchen with a well and shallow fireplace, specially designed to give off more heat than a deeper one would. During the summer season, museum guides bake biscuits in the "beehive oven."

Nearby, on the corner of King and Montague Streets, is the Ross Memorial Museum, a neoclassical brick building first occupied in 1824 by the Honourable Harris Hatch. Minister Henry Phipps Ross, and his wife, Sarah Juliette, daughter of the president of an important financier, bought the house in 1938. Their pictures grace the chandelier-lit hallway of the home. Thanks to Mrs. Ross's large inheritance, the couple travelled widely, returning

ABOVE: A view of Water Street wharf at low tide.

RIGHT: Sealife at your fingertips at the Huntsman Marine Science Centre.

each year with rare treasures of fine furniture, crystal, carpets and exotic animal skins. The spacious dining room contains massive mahogany furniture, including two writing desks and a bookcase. A spiral staircase leads to the white and peach master bedroom with a round table beautifully inlaid with mother-of-pearl, soapstone, jade and other semi-precious stones.

The Charlotte County Court House and Gaol, built in 1840, is a national historic site. It is New Brunswick's best preserved example of a typical mid-nineteenth-century courthouse and jail. The hand-carved royal coat of arms in the pediment was an artistic flourish added in 1858. The jail now houses an archive with the recorded history of Charlotte County.

The St. Andrews town wharf, just off Water Street, has long been a working wharf for scallop draggers, fishing boats and aquaculture barges. From here, visitors can head out into the Passamaquoddy Bay aboard a cutter, catamaran cruiser or racing Zodiac to watch whales. Touring the bay in a sea kayak is another exciting adventure. The Huntsman Marine Science Centre is named after Dr. Archibald Gowanlock Huntsman (1883–1973), who stimulated fishery research in the region. One of the attractions of the centre is the three harbour seals who are fed herring twice a day. Displays include a variety of local fish, such as halibut, lumpfish, sea cucumbers and baby lobsters.

ABOVE: The St. Andrews Blockhouse, erected in 1812.

BELOW: A path past the windmill in Kingsbrae Gardens.

Not far from the Huntsman Marine Science Centre is St. Andrews Blockhouse, erected as a coastal border defense during the War of 1812 and now a national historic site. It was built by townspeople in fear of an American invasion. This is one of twelve blockhouses in St. Andrews. They were quickly constructed, using local squared timber to form a structure about 6 metres (20 feet) square on the lower floor — the upper storey overhung almost a metre (3 feet) on each side. The sturdiness of this construction rendered them relatively secure against attack. In addition to the side gun ports and loopholes, holes were cut in the floor of the overhang to cover besiegers directly below.

St. Andrews's multi-award-winning attraction is the enchanting Kingsbrae Garden (Scottish for Kings Hill Garden), an 11-hectare (27-acre) site located at the top of the town. In 1996 the estate and property that form the garden were donated by John and Lucinda Flemer, who wanted to build a horticultural and cultural public garden to employ and train locals and attract visitors to the area. Today, it features

ABOVE: The Entry Garden at Kingsbrae Gardens, opened in 1996.

RIGHT: The rill (garden canal) at Kingsbrae Gardens.

more than 50,000 plants and flowers in traditional and modern garden styles and themes such as the Cottage Garden, Knot Garden, Perennial Garden, Therapy Garden, Secret Garden, Peace Garden, Sculpture Garden and the Children's Fantasy Garden. The horticultural showcase also features a cedar maze, two ponds, streams and a fully functioning small-scale Dutch windmill. The Acadian Forest Trail leads visitors among trees of the coastal region. Pygmy goats, peacocks, ducks and a family of alpacas are also a great attraction of the park. The Garden Café, overlooking a park with an ancient Persian canal fountain and modern statues, offers culinary delights that can be enjoyed out on the patio or inside, out of the sun. The Kingsbrae Garden was named Garden of the Year by the Canadian Garden Council Tourism Awards, 2013.

A view of Head Harbour Light Station.

③ CAMPOBELLO ISLAND

Museums and Historical Sites

- Roosevelt Cottage
- Hubbard Cottage

Parks

- Old Sow Whirlpool
- Roosevelt Campobello International Park
- Herring Cove Provincial Park
- Head Harbour Light Station

Close to the Maine border lies the island of Campobello. It remained the feudal fief of a dynasty of Welsh seamen until the late 1800s, among them Captain William Owen, who settled there in 1770 and named the scenic island Campobello. The Owen family sold most of their property in 1881 to a Boston realty firm. One shoreline lot was bought by the Delano family, whose daughter married a Roosevelt. Their son, Franklin Delano Roosevelt, better known as FDR, spent most of his boyhood summers here in a big cottage that has become Campobello's major tourist attraction. Connected to Lubec, Maine, by a highway bridge, Campobello has had a strong American link since the early twentieth century. The island remains a favourite vacation place for Americans. To reach Campobello from New Brunswick without travelling through Maine, first take the toll-free ferry from L'Etete to Deer Island, a small island with several attractions, such as small galleries, two lighthouses and the Old Sow Whirlpool, which has swallowed up a good number of boats. From southern

Deer Island, a car toll ferry connects to Campobello Island.

Franklin and Eleanor Roosevelt's summer home is a big estate with thirty-four rooms on 1.6 hectares (4 acres) of land, with a fine view of the Bay of Fundy. A tour of the red and green house offers a glimpse of Franklin Roosevelt's personality as he spent many summers there as a child. As a little boy he wrote to his mother that all he wanted for Christmas was "a box of blocks, and a train, and a little boat." He loved the island and became a passionate yachtsman. During a summer vacation with Eleanor and their children in August 1921, Roosevelt developed what was diagnosed as a severe cold after fighting a forest fire and then taking a dip in the icy waters of the bay. Unfortunately, a month later, he became partially paralyzed, and his condition was diagnosed as polio. He returned only a few times to the island from then on. He served as president of the United States from 1933 to 1945.

TOP: The exterior of Roosevelt Cottage.

INSET: A room with a view inside Hubbard Cottage.

The Roosevelt Campobello International Park is jointly administered by Canada and the United States. The park includes the Roosevelt Cottage, an interpretive centre, a leafy park with picnic tables, a hiking trail and the Hubbard Cottage. The Hubbards, friends of the Roosevelts, had a summer

A view of the falls and gorge in St. George, on the way to Campobello Island.

home nearby. Mr. Hubbard was an insurance broker from Boston.

On the ground floor of the Hubbards' house there is a bright and airy living room furnished in light oak. The dining room is notable not so much for its furniture as its unusual oval window and the beautiful view it offers of the bay.

The park service offers free Roosevelt and Hubbard Cottage tours, guided hikes with a naturalist, and Fantastic, Unbelievable, and definitely Not-ordinary (F.U.N.) Tours, which should not be missed. In another stately home, now a restaurant nearby, the park has a program called Eleanor's Tea where you'll enjoy tea, sandwiches and biscuits and hear about Mrs. Roosevelt's striving for human rights.

These cottages are by no means the only attractions on Campobello Island. The Roosevelt Campobello International Park and the adjacent Herring Cove Provincial Park both have scenic hiking trails along the coast to a bog and through shaded woodlands. Aside from hiking, visitors to the island spend time golfing, sea-kayaking, beachcombing and whale watching. A trip to the Head Harbour Light Station at the northern tip of the island is recommended. The view across to the lighthouse with the red cross is beautiful. A crude trail with steep ladders used to allow access to the lighthouse complex during low tide. Ladder support structures have deteriorated and access to the lighthouse is no longer possible. The ladders may be repaired in the future, but even without access, the view from the vista point to the lighthouse is just picture perfect.

TOP: A weir just off shore, with Swallowtail Lighthouse in the background.

INSET: The first ferry of the day arriving at dawn.

4 GRAND MANAN   

Museums and Historical Sites

- Grand Manan Museum
- Southwest Head Lighthouse
- Swallowtail Lighthouse

Arts and Culture

- Dark Harbour

Parks

- Red Point Beach
- Machias Seal Island
- Whale Cove

Grand Manan, the Queen of the Fundy Isles, has long been a haven for summer residents, both Canadian and American. But possibly the island's first visitors were from the Peskotomuhkati Nation, collecting eggs of gulls and other seabirds. They called it mananook, meaning "island place." In 1604, the French explorer Samuel de Champlain recorded seeking shelter here during a storm. He added the term "Grand" to "Manan," a French adaptation of the original name. Subsequently, the island changed hands a number of times between the French and the English, reflecting the fortunes of war on the faraway continent. In 1784, fifty United Empire Loyalist families arrived, and many of today's residents are descendants of these Loyalists. For a time, it was unclear whether Britain or the newly independent United States owned

A whale watching tour spotting its quarry.

the island. The boundary dispute was finally settled in 1842 in favour of the British.

Grand Manan's natural beauty and solitude has attracted naturalists, geologists, writers and artists over the last 200 years. The visit of John James Audubon to Grand Manan in the mid-nineteenth century has resulted in hundreds of birders coming to the island to look for rare birds among the 250 species that nest here. The feature exhibit in the museum on Grand Manan pays tribute to naturalist and taxidermist Allan Moses (1881–1953), whose collection includes a snowy owl, egrets, mergansers, teals, plovers and falcons.

Dr. Abraham Gesner conducted a geological survey on the island in 1839 and reported that the eastern area consists of 540- to 600-million-year-old Precambrian/Cambrian metamorphic rock, whereas the western part is formed by much younger, late Triassic, about 200-million-year-old volcanic rock, mostly basalt. The line where the two geological formations meet is clearly visible in the cliff face at Red Point Beach.

Buchanan Charles of North Andover, Massachusetts, founded the Grand Manan Historical Society in 1931, and his remarkable collection of historical material was later donated to the society's archives. American author Willa Cather (of *O, Pioneers!* fame) is one of the well-known writers who once called the island home.

Grand Manan, at the mouth of the Bay of Fundy, is wedge-shaped. The western shore is a sheer cliff more than 100 metres (328 feet) high and running the full 25-kilometre (16-mile) length of the island. The eastern side has a low contour, and is sheltered by other small islands. All the villages and roads are found on this protected eastern shore. Basically, there is a wilderness with high, forbidding cliffs on one side, spruce forest, streams and wetlands in the middle and a strip of settlement going back almost 220 years on the eastern side. Many of the hiking trails that wind along the western clifftops once served as life-saving paths — the number of shipwrecks around the island gave rise to a patrol-and-rescue path. Six lighthouses guard the archipelago against the dangerous ledges that stretch across the bay to the south and west. Thirteen kilometres (8 miles) out in the Bay of Fundy, the now defunct Gannet Rock Lighthouse has stood as guardian since 1831. A year later, a second lighthouse was erected at Machias Seal Island, located about a half-hour boat ride off Grand Manan, to guard the other end of the shipping hazard. Both New Brunswick and Maine claim Machias Seal Island; today the island is administered jointly. The island's puffin colony has drawn so many birders over the years that access had to be limited. Now a single group of Canadian visitors can spend the morning there, while the afternoon is reserved for a boatload of birdwatchers out of Eastport, Maine.

Swallowtail Lighthouse at North Head, Grand Manan, is located on a peninsula that offers spectacular views of herring weirs, fishing boats and sea birds. Every few hours the ferry from the mainland can be seen as it rounds the peninsula.

Whale Cove is a good vantage point to watch the seining of the weirs. The Jubilee Weir is visible from the Hole-in-the-Wall, the picturesque natural arch at the edge

The Hole-in-the-Wall rock formation.

A view from the hills down to the hamlet of Dark Harbour.

of a cliff near the old airstrip. The herring are caught in weirs off the coast of Grand Manan and packed for market at the last surviving sardine cannery in all of Canada and the United States, in Blacks Harbour. Due to the steady flushing action of the tides, Grand Manan has a lobster pound, where lobsters are kept in captivity until they are ready for market. Today, lobster fishing and salmon farming are two important industries on Grand Manan.

Dark Harbour, one of the most scenic parts of the island, is known for its dulse, an edible, reddish-purple seaweed, which is harvested at low tide, then spread out on a net on crushed rock to dry. On a sunny day, it dries in about five hours. The dulse leaves then stick to each other, and the harvest can be rolled like carpet. It first goes into storage, then is ground into flakes or powder. While chewing it raw is an acquired taste, it is also widely used as seasoning on fish, eggs and potato salad. The imposing cliffs, scenic views and breathtaking sunsets make Dark Harbour a must see.

4 EASTERN FUNDY COAST

Northumberland Strait
Confederation Bridge
PEI
Moncton
2
Fredericton
NOVA SCOTIA
9 Hillsborough
8 Hopewell Cape
7 Riverside-Albert
6 Mary's Point
5 Cape Enrage
4 Fundy National Park
114
111
Saint John River
Salmon River
Fundy Trail Parkway
3 St. Martins
Bay of Fundy
2 Willow Grove
1 Saint John

① SAINT JOHN

Museums and Historical Sites

- Fort Howe
- Firefighters Museum
- Carleton Martello Tower
- Trinity Anglican Church
- Loyalist House
- St. John's Stone Church
- Saint John Jewish Historical Museum and Shaarei Zedek Synagogue
- New Brunswick Museum
- Fort La Tour

Arts and Culture

- City Market
- Market Square
- John Hooper sculptures

Parks

- Irving Nature Park
- Saint John Skywalk and Reversing Falls
- Fallsview Park and Bridge

Saint John, Canada's first incorporated city, is situated where the mighty Saint John River meets the force of the Bay of Fundy tides. The city's site was once a traditional gathering place and village for the nomadic Wolastoqiyik people. Samuel de Champlain marked this place on his map after meeting the Wolastoqiyik and their chief on his short visit on June 24, 1604. Today, a statue of Samuel de Champlain

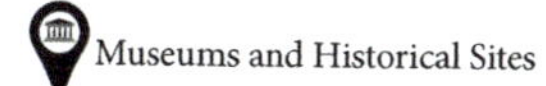
Museums and Historical Sites
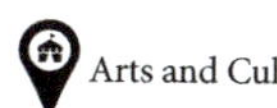
Arts and Culture

Parks

The river running out at the Reversing Falls, where the Saint John River meets the Bay of Fundy.

in Queen's Square memorializes his arrival and naming of the town over 400 years ago.

After the French lost possession of this region, the English erected Fort Howe, perched high above the city to protect the harbour from American privateers and other marauders. From 1785 on, the blockhouse served as the city's first jail. Today, the small, locked fort offers some nice views of the city and port.

A view of Partridge Island across Saint John Harbour.

The harbour witnessed the arrival of many frigates, "but never in its renowned and varied history did it behold such a scene as on May 11, 1783, when a number of little sailing craft winged their way up the Bay of Fundy, rounded Partridge Island, and dropped anchor to the salute of guns from Fort Howe," wrote historian H. A. Cody, describing the arrival of Loyalist refugees. From May to September 1783, more than 2,000 Loyalists arrived at the mouth of the Saint John River. They had fled their homes in the thirteen colonies at the end of the Revolutionary War, fearing prosecution for their loyalty to the Crown.

From 1785 to 1942, three million immigrants, mostly from eastern Europe and Ireland, landed on Partridge Island at the entrance of Saint John Harbour. In 1844, 2,000 Irish immigrants made their way to New Brunswick; 6,000 more arrived in 1845 and 9,000 in 1846. Most were destitute, and

The bandstand in King's Square, a public space since 1783.

because they were already weak from starvation, they were easy targets for typhus and other killer diseases. They were treated by a dedicated young physician who himself subsequently fell victim to the typhus fever. On the grounds of the small island, a Celtic cross commemorates the fever victims and Dr. Collins. Most survivors headed for the "Boston States," but some stayed in Saint John or moved up the Saint John River valley to settle there. The museum and other structures are now defunct and access to Partridge Island has been denied since the island was vandalized. Nature has reclaimed this island, and with it, one of Canada's best-kept historical secrets.

In 1783, as soon as Saint John's streets were laid out, the Loyalists began to build their homes. King's Square and Queen's Square were reserved as public places. The walkways across the squares formed the pattern of the Union Jack, which is

Fort Howe, erected by the British in 1785.

ABOVE: Carleton Martello Tower, erected during the War of 1812.

LEFT: Soldiers' cots inside the tower.

still evident. Several stores and houses were built between King's Square and the Public Landing, now Market Square, but on June 18, 1784, a fire destroyed many of the buildings.

In response to the fire and two years after Saint John was incorporated as a city in 1787, a system of fire protection was established. Wells were sunk and two fire engines purchased. This was the era of the hand pump — the first phase in mechanized firefighting. One of these old hand pumpers, a wagon with two long handles on its sides, is on display in the Firefighters Museum at King's Square. During a fire, six volunteers were stationed at each handle; they were able to operate two pistons that pumped the water through two hoses.

When the War of 1812 broke out and relations between Great Britain and the United States were strained, defensive measures were undertaken. Far on the west side of the city, on a rocky knoll, the mighty Carleton Martello Tower, a circular stone fortification, was erected. By the time the tower was finished the war was over, and

Trinity Anglican Church, opened in 1791 and rebuilt in 1880 after the Saint John Fire.

TOP: Loyalist House, built in 1817.

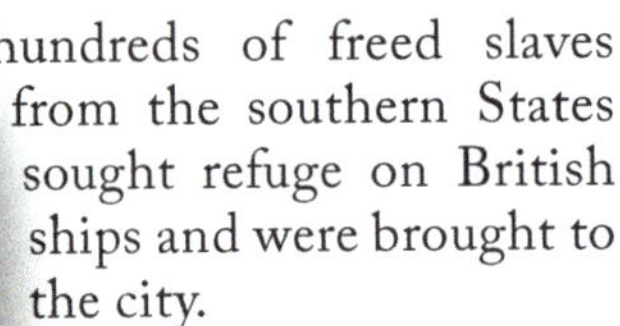

BELOW: Vase on display in Loyalist House.

hundreds of freed slaves from the southern States sought refuge on British ships and were brought to the city.

The Carleton Martello Tower, a national historic site, has recently undergone major renovations. The interior of the round structure consists of a single room with a large supporting pillar in the centre. Along the brick walls are the bedsteads of the soldiers, complete with folding cots, mattresses, pegs for their scarlet uniforms, canteens, and firearms. The basement is a heavily constructed powder storeroom. To reduce the risk of explosions, the only source of light was a single lantern. The site offers a good view of the city, the harbour and the Bay of Fundy.

In 1877 the Great Fire destroyed two thirds of Saint John, rendering 2,700 families homeless. Trinity Anglican Church, Saint John's first established congregation, which opened on Christmas Day, 1791, was also destroyed. Reconstruction of the city took many years. The church was replaced with the present brick and stone building in 1880 on its Germain Street location. The royal coat of arms, which survived the fire, is mounted inside over the west door. Today, Trinity Anglican Church is a national historic site.

Unlike practically all the houses of the late eighteenth and early nineteenth

ABOVE: Boston-style townhouses in the downtown core.

RIGHT: The Three Sisters lamp on Prince William Street, installed in 1848.

century in downtown Saint John, the Loyalist House, completed in 1817, was not destroyed by the Great Fire. Having fled the American Revolution, the United Empire Loyalist David Merritt and his family built this Georgian-style home on a corner lot of Germain and Union Streets. It is the oldest house in Saint John, now a museum. The house is meticulously furnished and decorated in a period no later than 1833, featuring wooden artistry by Thomas Nisbet on a poster bed and a serving table. The piano is more than it first appears: pull the right knob, push the appropriate pedal, and it becomes a pump organ. This Lemuel Gilbert piano with organ attachment is one of two left in the world and the only one that works! There is a Bible on the sewing table in the living room. Sunday was supposed to be the day of rest, but the sewing still had to be done. When the preacher came, the clothes went into the bag hanging from the table, the Bible was

St. John's Stone Church, built in 1824.

Yad Torah pointer on display at the Shaarei Zedek synagogue and Jewish Historical Museum.

opened, and everything was in order. Many historical items in this house stretch your imagination about their purpose. You may be amazed to find out that a wooden, mini wringer look-alike implement is a hand-cranked fluting iron that in the late 1800s was used to iron pleats and ruffles on collars and dresses.

St. John's Stone Church, another surviving structure of the Great Fire, dates back to 1824. Made from stone ballast used to fill the cargo of departing ships from England, the church has escaped destruction from fire four times. Its impressive stained-glass windows were imported from England, Germany and Ontario. The church is one of the first Gothic revival churches in Canada. It was designated a national historic site in 1987.

In 1858 the first Jewish family arrived in Saint John; by 1898 the community had grown significantly. A second wave of Jewish immigration at the turn of the century further boosted the community. Between 1920 and 1960 there were up to 300 Jewish families in Saint John. Some moved and made their fortune in Beverly Hills, like the famous Louis B. Mayer, the co-founder of Metro-Goldwyn-Mayer Studios. Others stayed and operated their own businesses or served in the armed forces in the Second World War. The Saint

Grotesques (stone carvings) on the Chubb Building.

Saint John City Market.

John Jewish Historical Museum is attached to an active synagogue. Photos and displays celebrate the city's Jewish heritage.

The city prospered from lumbering and shipbuilding. Reminders of the city's rich commercial heritage remain, including the historic brick warehouses; Boston-style townhouses; impressive homes of merchants, politicians and brewers; the former stock exchange; the first chartered bank, the Bank of New Brunswick with its massive, fluted columns; and the signs of the Jardine Shipping Line. The Seamen's Mission on Prince William Street and "the Three Sisters," a red and white streetlamp that has helped guide ships into the harbour since 1848, show another side of the city's seafaring heritage. It is no wonder that the Saint John City Market resembles the inverted hull of a boat, an appropriate symbol in a city made rich by shipbuilding. The design was the result of a competition among local architects. Since 1877, the market has been both a meeting place and a farmers' market for residents and visitors, offering a wide variety of crafts and foodstuffs — lobsters and dulse, meat and cheese, fruit, baked muffins and maple syrup. On your walk along Prince William Street at the Chubb's Corner building, you'll see stone carvings looking down to you. These sixteen grotesques were added when the burnt building was rebuilt after the 1877 fire. Two resemble actual people of that time: One was the city's mayor, S. Z. Earle Jr., who was tossed out of office after neglecting the

TOP: *Timepiece*, a sculpture by John Hooper at the entrance of Market Square.

LEFT: *People Apart Coming Together*, a Hooper sculpture in Market Square.

city's port rebuilding after the Great Fire. The other resembles one of the city's most eligible bachelors. One rumor asserts that the grotesques may have been created as revenge by a stone carver because his bosses did not pay him!

Like other Maritime centres, Saint John shared in the wartime booms of 1914 and 1939. A local entrepreneur, K. C. Irving, moved to Saint John to establish a car dealership and went on to build an industrial empire that transformed the province's economy. By 1949, he owned the region's largest bus carrier, all the English-language daily newspapers in Saint John and Moncton (he purchased the last remaining large newspaper in Fredericton

TOP: An American mastodon skeleton at the New Brunswick Museum.

RIGHT: A minke whale skeleton at the museum.

in 1968), several sawmills, a paper mill, vast forest holdings, Saint John Dry Dock and an ever-expanding string of service stations, selling products from the Irving refinery at Saint John. By the 1990s, the second and third generations of Irvings were carrying on the family tradition. The Irvings' tribute to the people of Saint John is the Irving Nature Park on the Taylor Peninsula, an eco-tourism site with charming nature trails near and along the shore.

Nestled in the restored Market Square amongst shops, pubs and cafés, you'll find two wooden sculptures by John Hooper, *Timepiece* and *People Apart Coming Together*, as well as fountains, the public library and the New Brunswick Museum. The museum boasts amazing displays that bring the province's natural history alive. It features geological displays and the Hall of Great Whales. The preserved fossil bones of a huge American mastodon, trapped in mud and found in a New Brunswick lake in 1936, are displayed in skeleton form on the second floor. This fossil is one of the most complete mastodons found in the Maritimes. The skeletons of a rare northern right whale, a

ABOVE: The tide coming in at Reversing Falls.

LEFT: The welcome sign at the Reversing Falls Skywalk.

sperm whale and a minke whale are impressive displays of sea mammals found in the Bay of Fundy in summer months. Upstairs is also a gallery with fine and decorative art.

Reversing Falls is a famous natural attraction in Saint John. An information centre complete with video presentations, a viewing platform and a skywalk is located on a steep cliff overlooking the Saint John River near its mouth. When the tide is going out, the river empties into the Bay of Fundy. It does so quite vigorously; there are pools and eddies, and it is not safe for boats

A view of Saint John Harbour.

to run the rapids. After the tide turns and the water in the bay rises, the pressure of the river water flowing down and the water of the bay pushing up is equal. This is low slack tide, and it is safe for boats to pass through — but only for twenty minutes. After that, the water of the bay rises so intensely that it actually pushes the water upriver. For about six hours, water flows upstream. At high slack tide, boats can briefly pass through the narrows until the tide joins the river current, creating turbulent rapids at the river's mouth. Another excellent viewpoint of the Reversing Falls is across from the visitor centre at the other end of the bridge at Fallsview Park.

The new national historic site Fort La Tour was set to open in June 2021. On the night of May 19, Saint John firefighters were called to stop a suspicious fire at the site. The damage to the replica was extensive, but fortunately, the site was rebuilt. Fort La Tour is located at the mouth of the Saint John River within Saint John Harbour. It resembles the fort that the Acadian governor La Tour had erected here in 1631 as a fur trade centre for Acadians and Indigenous people of the area. Inside, you learn about Madame de La Tour's bravery in 1645 during her husband's absence. The New Brunswick liquor producer Sébastien Roy honoured the Acadian La Tour and his wife by calling his newest brandy "Fort La Tour," and Cy, a group of Moncton musicians, produced a song about the La Tours. The small park around the site offers good views along with some statues and grassy areas with benches.

② WILLOW GROVE

Museums and Historical Sites

- Willow Grove Baptist Church and Monument

TOP: Willow Grove Baptist Church.

INSET: Willow Grove monument.

Along the Fundy Coastal Drive, in Willow Grove, east of the Saint John airport, a white and black chapel and a monument stand as reflections of Black New Brunswickers' history. Starting in 1813, the British military promised to free enslaved Blacks in America in exchange for allegiance to the English Crown, offering those freed land to settle in British North America or the West Indies. Of these Black Loyalists, 2,000 settled in Nova Scotia, and 371 settled in the Loch Lomond-Willow Grove area near Saint John in 1816. They received a land grant of 22 hectares (55 acres) in 1836, but were intentionally given smaller plots of lower quality land than white Loyalists that also came, making survival difficult. Former British headmaster Edmund Duval was one of few white settlers at the time to support the Black population's advocacy for the improvement of their social and economic conditions in New Brunswick society. Duval bought a farm in the area of Willow Grove and shared farming techniques with residents.

Despite discriminatory treatment the Willow Grove community persevered and their church, opened in 1878 with Duval's aid, still stands today. Descendents of the Black Loyalists who settled in Willow Grove still live in the Saint John area. In 2021, Canada Post commemorated Willow Grove on a postage stamp.

St. Martins Covered Bridge.

③ ST. MARTINS   

Museums and Historical Sites

- St. Martins covered bridges

Arts and Culture

- Big Salmon River Interpretive Centre

Parks

- Fundy Trail Parkway
- Walton Glen Gorge and Falls
- Flowerpot Footpath
- Goose River Trail
- Big Salmon River Suspension Bridge

Further east along Route 111 is the town of St. Martins, the gateway to the famous Fundy Trail Parkway. The small seaside community has two of the last remaining covered bridges at its active, picturesque harbour. The village also features reddish sea caves carved out by the powerful tidal waves. People can walk to these natural wonders at low tide (beach sandals are recommended) or view them from the small village beach at high tide. Organized kayaking tours to the sea caves are also popular here. Visitors may also want to taste St. Martin's famous seafood chowder and lobster rolls.

The Fundy Trail Parkway is a 30-kilometre (19-mile) coastal drive on a chip-sealed road from the outskirts of St. Martins to the Walton Glen Gorge area south of Sussex. The gated parkway leads through one of the last remaining coastal wilderness areas between Florida and Labrador. To protect its coastal ecosystem of nutrient-rich salt marshes, tidal flats and high Fundy tides, the

Sea Caves.

ABOVE: Visitor centre on the Fundy Trail Parkway.

LEFT: On the Fundy Footpath.

Fundy escarpment requires a 2-kilometre (1.25-mile) wide corridor along the Fundy coast: 1 kilometre (0.6 miles) on land and 1 kilometre (0.6 miles) into the bay.

Along the Fundy Trail Parkway are more than thirty viewpoints and observation decks. Visitors have access to sandy and rocky beaches, cliffs, flowerpot formations, waterfalls and a suspension bridge across the Big Salmon River at the former lumbering and shipbuilding community with the same name. In Long Beach a beautiful, wide, sandy beach stretches out over 2.5 kilometres (1.5 miles). Here, the tides go out for half a kilometre or about a quarter mile.

The Fundy Trail Parkway also features the Walton Glen Gorge. Due to its size and magnificent canyon, the area is known as the Grand Canyon of New Brunswick. A short, easy walk leads to a platform to allow great views into the canyon and across to the Walton Glen Falls, the second-largest waterfall in the province. Down in the gorge is the Eye of the Needle, where the walls close in from both sides with a brook running between them.

The parkway has a multi-use trail system for biking, walking and wheelchair use. There are also some interesting hiking trails, such as the scenic 3-kilometre (1.9-mile) return Flowerpot Footpath and the 1.4-kilometre (0.9-mile) return Long Beach Brook Falls leading to a waterfall. The long-distance Fundy Footpath is a strenuous four to five day backpacking trip. It starts at the Big Salmon River suspension bridge and leads along the rugged Fundy coast via the Goose River Trail to the parking lot at Point Wolfe in Fundy National Park. Before venturing out, hikers need to sign up at the Big Salmon River Interpretive Centre.

Sea Stack near the coast.

4 FUNDY NATIONAL PARK

Museums and Historical Sites	Arts and Culture	Parks
• Point Wolfe Covered Bridge	• Town of Alma • Point Wolfe Campground	• Coastal Trail • Dickson Falls Trail

Fundy National Park, Fundy for short, covers a natural region of 206 square kilometres (80 square miles), laid out in a rectangle roughly 13 by 16 kilometres (8 by 10 miles).

Here the Acadian forest of the Caledonia Highlands meets the great tides of the Bay of Fundy. The highway through the park is steeper than most roads in southern New Brunswick. The Butland Lookout on Route 114 just before the road tumbles down to sea level provides a memorable view of the blue waters far below. The park's landmark is the red covered bridge at Point Wolfe along the Coastal Route.

Fundy boasts a variety of ecosystems: from the windswept cliffs and sandy beaches along the bay to large stands of beautiful hardwoods; from boggy swamps to deep gorges with roaring waterfalls. The famous Fundy tides reach heights between 9 and 12 metres (30 to 40 feet) and the tides can be seen in action at Point Wolfe Beach, Herring Cove Beach and in Alma, the charming village adjoining the park.

Founded in 1948 to protect the region's natural and cultural heritage, the park manages wildlife and ecological programs, and the park rangers offer interpretive walks and evening events. As a result of active conservation efforts, there are now more adult salmon returning to the Fundy rivers than have in three decades. Hikers may want to

Museums and Historical Sites Arts and Culture Parks

ABOVE: Fundy National Park, covered bridge.

BELOW: Beaver.

look for salmon on the Upper Salmon River Trail in the river's clear salmon pond areas.

Irish, Scottish and English settlers in the early 1800s made their homes along the bay to take advantage of the fertile lands. Those settling in the cold highlands along Shepody Road, which now forms the northern border of the park, were faced with misery and hardship, because the soil was rocky and the growing season too short. They soon had to abandon their farms and move to the milder area near the coast. There, however, the good lots had already been claimed. Many families settled in Herring Cove and in what is now the village of Alma. The best farmland in Fundy was found in the high-priced lots along the coast where rivers and brooks entered the Bay of Fundy. John Matthew was one of the first to arrive, and he obtained a land grant at Herring Cove. His farm and his son's neighbouring farm flourished. Remains of the former Matthew homestead with rock foundations can be found by hiking down to Matthews Head.

Between Matthews Head and Alma near today's swimming pool, Otis Cannon built and operated a small sawmill and a tide-powered fishing weir. At the western park boundary, the Point Wolfe River and

ABOVE: Grounded fishing boats at low tide in Alma.

RIGHT: The ghost plant (*Monotropa uniflora*).

the Goose River were once the major sites of water-powered lumber mills. By 1826, the mill town of Point Wolfe was founded, wharves were constructed in the estuary and the virgin forest was harvested to build the city of Saint John. Today, the Goose River Trail crosses a small brook called Schoolhouse — the only reminder of the settlement at Goose River. Further logging activity was carried out upriver, evident on the East Branch Loop. Part of the trail uses a former hauling road, which leads to the remains of an old logging dam at the East Branch River. In the nineteenth century, red spruce trees and stately white pines were hauled to the East Branch and floated down to the sawmill at Point Wolfe.

The people who settled this region are long gone and their homesteads and fields have been reclaimed by forests as wilderness is allowed to return. Despite the aggressive harvesting of red spruce up until the park's foundation, remnants of older red spruce still stand. They are characteristic of the Maritimes' Acadian forest, a mixed forest with signature species that include red spruce, eastern hemlock, eastern white pine,

Dickson Falls.

Goose River Trail.

sugar maple, red oak and others. Old growth can still be seen along the Coastal Trail that starts at Point Wolfe. A climb leads to the big red spruce trees distinguished by their rust-coloured twigs. Some virgin red spruce, up to 350 years old, may still exist in steep stream valleys that are difficult to harvest.

Under the conifers, there are ferns, mosses and other shade-tolerant plants that sprout from the acid soil, including bunchberries, wood sorrel, clintonia lily, wild sarsaparilla, wild lily-of-the-valley, twinflower and the white ghost plant. Yellow birch, maple and beech trees form the beautiful hardwood ridges found in Fundy. Trout lily, red trillium and red elderberry mixed with ferns blanket the forest floor. Painted and white trillium, pink lady's slipper orchid, the starflower and many fungi prefer this forest. Nurse logs line the trails: Hardwood seedlings sprout in the moist soil provided by fallen, decomposing trees. Some of these new trees will have long exposed roots, well off the ground, a sign that they grew atop a log, which rotted away over time.

Fundy National Park offers a range of activities from camping, hiking, biking and mountain biking to paddling and bird watching, fishing and golf, as well as swimming in a heated saltwater pool. The choice of trails in the park varies from easy to strenuous: from the short scenic Dickson Falls Trail and the beaver activity at MacLaren Pond Trail to the moderate to strenuous Upper Salmon River Trail and Coastal Trail. The moderately difficult Goose River Trail in the park connects with the demanding, multi-day Fundy Footpath outside the park boundaries.

The park offers regular campsites for tenting, fully serviced camper-style sites, backcountry campsites and also rustic cabins, yurts, oTENTiks that are part tent, part cabin, and the unusual Ôasis, a very small house with a futon and a hammock, at Point Wolfe Campground. The picturesque village of Alma offers accommodations, a variety of restaurants and a small grocery store.

As you visit and stay in the park, remember that coyotes, deer, moose, black bears, raccoons and beavers live in the park. Encounters with wild animals can be enjoyed and are safe, provided that campers keep a safe distance, keep their campsites clean and do not attempt to feed the animals.

Rapelling down the cliffs.

⑤ CAPE ENRAGE

Museums and Historical Sites

- Lighthouse

Arts and Culture

- Outdoor activities

Parks

- Cape Enrage cliffs

Not far from the Fundy National Park is the picturesque Cape Enrage, a steep, rocky cliff. The area invites exhilarating activities such as rappelling, kayaking and zip lining, and less strenuous activities, such as searching for fossils on the shore at low tide or just enjoying the scenery around the lighthouse.

Sandpipers on their migratory route.

⑥ MARY'S POINT

Arts and Culture

- Mary's Point Shorebird Centre

At Mary's Point, between mid-July and early August, hundreds of thousands of shorebirds rest on their migratory route. The short Beach Trail slopes down from the Mary's Point Shorebird Centre to the beach and offers the best vantage point for observing the birds. Sandpipers and plovers of various subspecies congregate here on the mudflats after the tide goes out. They feed on tiny mud shrimps and worms. Well-fed and rested, the birds are ready for the four-day flight to their winter habitat in northern South America. Among the birds that roost on the beach is the semipalmated plover, a chubby little bird with a single black band across its white breast. Its flying and roosting companions are the fairly large, orange-legged ruddy turnstone and the semipalmated sandpiper.

One minute the flock roosts and the next, amidst a sudden wave of flashing dark and silvery light, a dense clump of birds arcs swiftly into the air along the shore, gracefully shifting this way and that. Then they settle down on the beach and repeat their spectacular performance a little while later. A truly amazing natural show. Another important migratory site is located across Shepody Bay at Dorchester Cape.

Crooked Creek Lookout.

⑦ RIVERSIDE-ALBERT

Parks

- Crooked Creek Trail and Lookout
- Caledonia Mountain

Taking Route 114 south towards Alma, you will pass through the village of Riverside-Albert. In town, the Crooked Creek hiking trail leads through softwoods to viewpoints across the Shepody Marsh and Riverside-Albert and further up to a stunning lookout platform across a forested ravine on Caledonia Mountain. The 3.2-kilometre (2-mile) return trail is moderately difficult and especially rewarding in the fall with its blazing maple ridges. If you have less energy or time, driving up the Crooked Creek Road also leads to the lookout.

Low tide at the Hopewell Rocks.

8 HOPEWELL CAPE

Museums and Historical Sites

- Albert County Museum

Parks

- Hopewell Rocks

The Bay of Fundy is known for the highest tides in the world. The amazing Hopewell Rocks in Hopewell Cape are shaped as flowerpot rocks by the immense tides. Twice a day, one hundred billion tonnes of salt water makes its way in and out of the Bay of Fundy. The rise and fall of the ocean is the result of the gravitational forces of the sun and moon. The tidal effects are the same all over the world, but here they are more visible due to the length and shape of the bay, which acts as a funnel, pushing the water inward. As there is no exit, the water level rises dramatically. The average change in water level at Hopewell Rocks is 10.7 metres (35 feet), the equivalent of a four-storey house. The largest change ever measured there was 14.8 metres (48.6 feet).

High tide at the Hopewell Rocks.

Low tide at the Hopewell Rocks.

In addition to whales and other sea mammals, thousands of shorebirds rest here among some unique geological formations, enjoying the benefits of the highest tides in the world. Many tours await adventurous types in the Fundy area. From late spring to late summer, travellers can watch finback whales, humpbacks, minkes and right whales up close. There is certainly nothing like the Bay of Fundy anywhere else.

The iconic Hopewell Rocks can best be experienced during both low and high tides. Indeed, tickets for the place are good for two days. At low tide, the fascination of Hopewell Rocks immediately becomes apparent as you gaze down the cliff and then walk down the three flights of metal stairs onto the ocean floor, around the base of the famous flowerpot rock formations, now towering towards the sky. Some of the ocean floor is soft, wet sand, some is mud with tidal pools, and some is rock. The reef is a surprisingly solid conglomerate rock. The exposed surface is blanketed with barnacles, small cone-shaped shells. Next to them grows rockweed, a curious seaweed with small oval bladders at its tips. At high tide, the ocean floor has filled up with water again, covering the foot of the flowerpot rocks and one flight of stairs as well. Visitors may want to sea kayak along the shore with an organized group or just watch the yellow, orange and red kayaks as they paddle through the maze of small rock islands.

A short distance from Hopewell Rocks on Route 114 is the Albert County Museum complex, including the courthouse, jail, Silver Jubilee Library and other buildings of the former shiretown (capital city). The stately county courthouse was built in 1904 to replace the original 1846 building, which burned down in 1902. The prominent style is classical revival. The courthouse features Douglas fir woodwork and the fancy, unusual ceiling decoration of pressed tin. The courtroom contains a prisoner's dock, witness stand, raised seating area and a public gallery.

Across from the courthouse is the former

jail with massive 66-centimetre (26-inch) walls, and 7.5-centimetre (3-inch) iron bars on the windows. Particularly chilling is the dungeon — a cell used for solitary confinement with a big iron ring in the centre to which unruly prisoners in leg irons were anchored. The wooden door has an axe mark: It played a part in one of the most famous murder trials in the country, the so-called "Rectory Murder." In December 1906, the housekeeper of the parish priest was brutally murdered in the course of an attempted robbery, while the priest was out of town. Evidence seemed to point to Tom Collins, a young man who had come from Ireland only months before. He had worked as handyman around the rectory near Riverside-Albert. The fascinating story is retold by Ken Saunders in *The Rectory Murder*.

TOP: Inside the courthouse at the Albert County Museum.

ABOVE: Exterior of the courthouse at the museum.

The adjacent large barn contains a lot of farm equipment, including a stump harrow, treadmill and butter churns. One of the more unusual items is a dog treadmill.

The table set for a meal at Steeves House Museum.

9 HILLSBOROUGH

Museums and Historical Sites

- Steeves House Museum
- New Brunswick Railway Museum

In the heart of Albert County lies Hillsborough, a village known for its historical trains and as the birthplace of William Henry Steeves. New Brunswick's only surviving steam engine and coach car is now permanently stationed to visit at Hillsborough's small New Brunswick Railway Museum. The museum also offers a display of locomotives, railway cars, and railroad memorabilia.

On 40 Mill Street in Hillsborough stands the white-panelled, Georgian-style Steeves House. William Henry Steeves, who was the owner of a shipbuilding company and grocery store, and who later became one of the Fathers of Confederation, was born in this house in 1814. During his years as a politician, Steeves supported the Intercolonial Railway and Confederation to further strengthen New Brunswick's economy. His parents, Heinrich and Rachel Stieff, had immigrated from Germany to Pennsylvania in 1749 and in 1766 came with a small group of settlers to this area at the Petitcodiac River. Their last name was later anglicized to Steeves. The museum guide will point out remodeled furniture and ingenious implements in the home. The living room is furnished with both a desk fashioned from a pump organ and an unaltered Estey pump organ from the Hillsborough Baptist Church.

The staircase has an unusual feature: a number of steps have prisms in them. Whenever the lady of the house required maid service, she would place a lantern beneath the stairs. The light shone through the prism, signaling the maid, who lived upstairs. The upstairs exhibits include a rope bed in the children's room. The rope had to be made taut each night, otherwise the bed would sag, thus giving rise to the saying, "good night, sleep tight."

5 SOUTHEASTERN ACADIAN COAST

ACADIAN COASTAL DRIVE

The Acadian Coastal Drive totals 477 kilometres (300 miles) from Aulac to Campbellton. Its southern part winds its way up the Acadian Peninsula along the scenic red- and white-sanded coastline of the Northumberland Strait. The strait is famous for its sandy beaches and some of the warmest salt water north of Virginia. For centuries, the strait has been a barrier between New Brunswick and Prince Edward Island.

Kayaking on the Northumberland Strait.

Downtown Moncton.

① MONCTON  

Museums and Historical Sites

- Moncton Museum - Resurgo Place
- Free Meeting House
- Thomas Williams House

Arts and Culture

- Butterfly World
- Magnetic Hill Zoo

Parks

- Bore Park
- Magnetic Hill

The Acadians' ancestors came to this region from western France between 1632 and 1635. They settled on the shores of the Petitcodiac River near an old Mi'kmaw portage site. They gradually developed self-sufficient agricultural communities along the Bay of Fundy, where fertile marshes and high tides ensured healthy grain surpluses for trade with New England. With the construction of Halifax and other English settlements as an answer to France's strengthened military posts in Nova Scotia (which, at that time, included what is now New Brunswick), the British considered the Acadian communities a threat to stability. In 1755, they decided to drive the Acadians from their homes. Fourteen thousand Acadians had to either swear allegiance to the British king or leave. Many of them left their homes and found their way to New England, Quebec, France, Prince Edward Island, the Magdalen Islands and in the course of time to the southern colonies. In 1758, a proclamation issued throughout the British colonies invited settlers to claim the unoccupied Acadian farmlands.

When the British government permitted the Acadian exiles to return in 1764, providing they dispersed throughout the area, they found their lands taken and many went further up the coast to Chaleur Bay in northern New Brunswick. The Moncton area at the Petitcodiac River was settled by the British and French in 1733, but

The incoming tidal bore viewed at Bore Park.

"the Bend," as it was called then, was officially founded in 1766 with the arrival of eight families from Pennsylvania, mostly of German descent. They settled at "the Bend of the Petitcodiac," where a memorial is erected at the landing site. Some of these German pioneer families and permanent settlers were named Trites (Treitz), Steeves (Stieff) and Lutes (Lutz) — surnames that are frequently found on mailboxes in the Sackville-Moncton area today.

In the 1840s, shipbuilding became a prosperous industry in Moncton. Mayor and shipbuilder Joseph Salter oversaw the building of twenty wooden sailing vessels during this boom time. The economic collapse, however, came in the 1860s. In the 1870s, the economy rebounded due to the Intercolonial Railway of Canada, who had set up their headquarters in Moncton. Moncton remained a railway town until the closure of the locomotive shops in the late 1980s. Moncton was able to recover from these two economic disasters and became a strong, enterprising city again, who proudly presents its town's logo "Resurgo" (Latin for "I rise again"). Today, Moncton is the largest city in New Brunswick, with a population of 72,000 (city) and 141,000 (metro).

Moncton's oldest surviving building is the Free Meeting House, a national historic site, located next to the city museum. Its spartan interior consists of grey box pews and a raised pulpit. Built in 1821 and true to its name, it has served as a home for Baptists, Methodists, Presbyterians, Roman Catholics, Reformed Episcopalians, Free Christian Baptists, Reformed Presbyterians, Seventh Day Adventists, Jews, Pentecostals and the Christian Science Church until such time as they were financially able to build their own church.

The Moncton Museum features the history of the city from the age of sail to the age of rail to the present. One particularly noteworthy artifact is a railway wheelbarrow made of butternut wood on the outside with birdseye maple as interior lining. Another exhibit provides historical information on dike building, including a display of tools.

Thomas Williams, the treasurer of the Intercolonial Railway, lived with his wife and eleven children in an 1883 Victorian Gothic-style house on Park Street. Today, Thomas Williams House is operated by the City of Moncton. The front porch tea room

TOP: Barn owls in their enclosure at the Magnetic Hill Zoo.

LEFT: A giant owl butterfly at Butterfly World.

and decor make this a lovely place to visit. One of the prettiest parts of the house is the upstairs hallway with its hardwood floors and alcove. On the rooftop are the ragged remains of once-elegant wrought iron cresting. The story goes that while Mr. and Mrs. Williams were away, one of their sons developed a craving for candy. Finding none in the house, he climbed onto the roof, took down some part of the cresting that he could reach and sold it to a junkman to get money to buy treats!

Bore Park in downtown Moncton offers a fine view of the tidal bore, a natural phenomenon caused twice daily when the tides of the Bay of Fundy begin to make their way up the Petitcodiac River. Depending on the position of the moon and sun, the tidal wave may be either a small upsurge or a flood wave. On average, the height of the tidal bore ranges from 0.5 metres (1 foot) to 1 metre (3 feet). This spectacular scene is worth observing as this incoming rush of water overtakes the outgoing tide in the placid river.

Another natural phenomenon is the Magnetic Hill in Moncton. Here, a stretch of dirt road appears to be sloping downwards. Guides direct cars to the "bottom" of the road, from where they roll backwards "up" to where they came from, a "magic" illusion.

Butterfly World on Mountain Road houses a small exhibit of butterflies in a building in the shape of a geo dome. Colourful flowers and slices of oranges attract the blue morpho, zebra, postman and other butterflies for close-up views.

The Magnetic Hill Zoo nearby features hundreds of animals in a leafy 16-hectare (40-acre) park: Amur tigers, plains zebras, dromedary camels, black bears, collared peccaries, marabou storks, barn owls, Caribbean flamingoes and many more. Zookeepers will show and discuss animals in their care at a certain time daily. You can either explore the premises on your own or take one of the one-hour tours offered by the zoo.

Sainte-Anne-de-Beaumont Chapel, built in 1842.

② MEMRAMCOOK

Museums and Historical Sites

Sainte-Anne-de-Beaumont Chapel

Between Moncton and the New Brunswick–Nova Scotia border, northeast of the Petitcodiac River in the Memramcook Valley, is the small Sainte-Anne-de-Beaumont Chapel, which was erected in 1842 by Acadians and the Mi'kmaq, who had converted to Catholicism. Three generations later, only four families remained in Beaumont; most left for Dorchester or the Fort Folly Reserve, but Sunday mass was still celebrated in the chapel during the summer months. In the 1990s, the church was vandalized and fell into a state of disrepair.

According to the history books, one evening in May of 1996, Father Sylvio Doiron entered the chapel and experienced a sudden inner sadness, noticing the dismal state of the place. Thanks to his leadership, the chapel and side building were revived. Today recognized as a provincial historic site, four flags are raised here: the Canadian, New Brunswick, Acadian and Mi'kmaq flag. Situated on a small hill, the site overlooks the picturesque banks of the Petitcodiac River and its dikes that were also built jointly by the Mi'kmaq and Acadians. Musical events and historical re-enactments are held in the chapel and on the chapel grounds during the summer.

The summer kitchen at Keillor House Museum.

③ DORCHESTER

Museums and Historical Sites

- Keillor House Museum
- St. James Textile Museum

Parks

- Dorchester Cape

Located between Memramcook and Sackville, the town of Dorchester overlooks the scenic Shepody Bay. At the Keillor House Museum the guides tell interesting stories of the Yeoman family, who worked as farm hands after their arrival from England. In the second generation, John Keillor rose to the status of sire and later justice of the peace. The Keillors offered free acres of land to the existing county administration, which was not centrally located. Their land ran conveniently along the main road in Dorchester. It was equipped with a tavern to encourage moving the county seat to the "shiretown" of Dorchester. With this move came businesses, lawyers, a federal prison and jail. The rail line and hotel came to Dorchester just after Confederation in 1867 by someone's dubious influence. The penitentiary collection shows intriguing artifacts, such as the selection of orthotic cobbler shoe molds made by inmates. They were of high quality and popular. The old jail across from the Keillor House is now a bed and breakfast, jailhouse-style!

Nearby is the St. James Textile Museum, showing artifacts of home textile production of woolen and linen fabrics, important for New Brunswick's rural economy in the nineteenth century. Visitors will also see weavers working on loom crofts.

Just to the south, at Dorchester Cape, thousands of semipalmated sandpipers rest and feed at the inter-tidal mudflats of the Shepody Bay during their migration in mid-July to early August: an amazing spectacle! A small interpretive centre near the observation site gives insight into the shorebirds' flocking behavior and flight routes, their predators, choice of food, special features and quantity.

④ SACKVILLE

Museums and Historical Sites

- Fort Beauséjour - Fort Cumberland National Historic Site

Arts and Culture

- Live Bait Theatre

Parks

- Sackville Waterfowl Park

Sackville is a town for fine and performing arts, reflecting Mount Allison University's specialties. Live Bait Theatre and summer concerts in the park, along with art galleries and craft shops give this town a special flare.

Downtown, on Main Street, you will see an unusual bronze man sitting on a bench holding a maple leaf design in his hands. The life-size sculpture was made by Christian Toth in memory of the Honourable George Stanley, who designed the Canadian flag in 1964. Stanley was born in Calgary in 1907. He worked as a professor and administrator at Mount Allison University in the 1930s and 1970s. He died in Sackville in 2002 and was immortalized here in 2018.

Sackville Waterfowl Park features a wooden boardwalk around a lake and a small covered bridge. Over the years, the cattails and other water plants have taken over parts of the lake. Not far from Sackville, on the provincial border with Nova Scotia, is the site of a fortress where two nations once fought for dominance in North America. Perched on a hill, Fort Beauséjour – Fort Cumberland overlooks the vast marshlands and dikes. In the early 1750s, England began building forts throughout Nova Scotia to protect its settlements. One was Fort Lawrence, of which no structure remains. The French quickly responded by building a neighbouring fort — Fort Beauséjour.

In 1754, a secretary at Fort Beauséjour informed the British about French military plans. The British decided to attack first. When the French learned about the impending attack, they sent an appeal for help to Fortress Louisbourg at the northern tip of Nova Scotia. At the same time, they prepared for the attack by burning all wooden structures that might ignite

Statue of Dr. Stanley, designer of the Canadian flag, in downtown Sackville.

The boardwalk at Sackville Waterfowl Park.

under cannon fire. The British launched an attack from thirty-eight boats that sailed up Chignecto Bay, carrying 2,000 militia, along with cannons and supplies. In early June, the British began their siege by digging trenches and bringing cannons into position. News arrived from Fortress Louisbourg that no reinforcements would be sent, and when a direct hit destroyed one of Fort Beauséjour's casements, the French surrendered. The victorious British forces renamed the structure Fort Cumberland. This imperial conflict brought about the expulsion of over 5,000 Acadians in 1755.

Fort Cumberland was prominent again during the American Revolutionary War when a small group of revolutionaries attacked it. The same summer, 200 Yorkshire settlers arrived to restore the damaged fort and defend the British colony against American forces.

In 1926, the fortress was declared a national historic site. Visitors can walk on the fort's star-shaped walls and look out across the marshes and dikes or explore the somber stone casements and barracks. Some plaques with images of paintings by Lewis Parker show scenes from 1754 to 1778 that illustrate life at the fort back then.

An answer to pandemic restrictions, Levee on the Lake is a late summer music and storytelling festival. Designed for people of all ages, the stage faces Silver Lake, inviting attendees to either lay down a blanket on the grass or "paddle in" and enjoy the show from the water!

A view of the Confederation Bridge from Cape Jourimain.

5 CAPE JOURIMAIN

Parks

- Confederation Bridge
- Cape Jourimain Nature Centre

Before the ferry and the Confederation Bridge, people crossed the strait from Cape Traverse to the mainland at Cape Jourimain by small open boats in the summer and ice-boats in winter. It was hard, dangerous work to paddle the exposed boats in open water, drag them through floating ice chunks and haul them like sleds over solid ice. For decades, Cape Tormentine, an outcrop near Cape Jourimain, has been the home of the New Brunswick ferry service to the island.

Plans for a permanent link were made three times after Confederation. After ten years of studies and court challenges, public hearings and plebiscites, the mega-bridge was finally built and was operational as of May 1997. The aptly named Confederation Bridge, celebrated as the largest saltwater bridge in the western hemisphere, connects the island and the mainland by a two-lane highway that is 11 metres (36 feet) wide. The "fixed link," as it is often called, stretches more than 13 kilometres (8 miles) across the sea. The structure is raised in its middle section, reaching a height of 64 metres (210 feet).

The Cape Jourimain Nature Centre at the mainland base of the Confederation Bridge offers the best vantage points for the bridge and the lighthouse either from the four-storey tower or along the short Lighthouse Trail. An interactive exhibit hall features displays on ecology, history, climate, transportation and 170 species of birds.

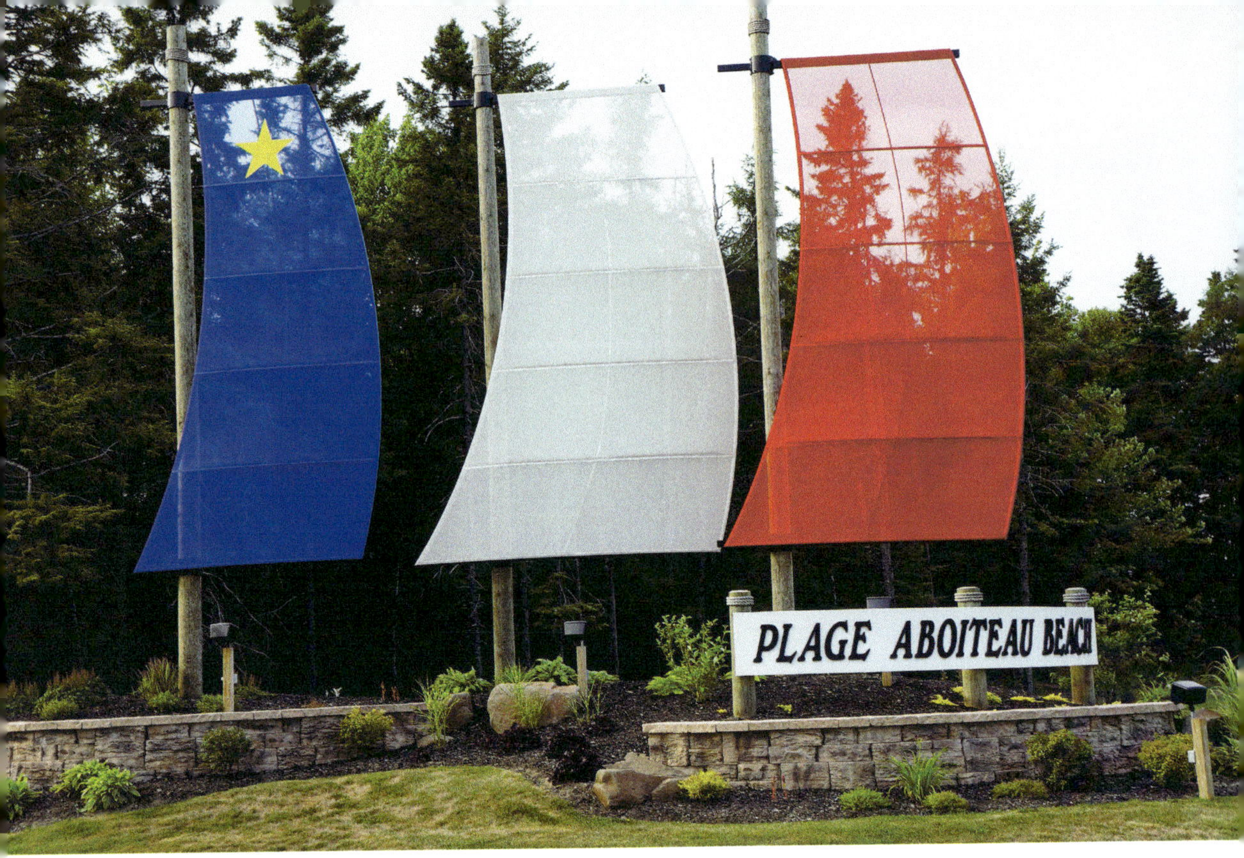

Aboiteau Beach and complex.

6 CAP-PELÉ

Parks

- Aboiteau Beach complex

Up the scenic coast is Cap-Pelé with its beautiful beaches and low tide sandbars that keep the water warm in summer. The Aboiteau Beach complex at Cap-Pelé includes a small vacation village with board-walks and bright wooden cottages that adorn the shore.

Lobster statue in winter, Shediac.

7 SHEDIAC

Arts and Culture

- Shediac Lobster Festival
- Concerts in the Park
- Music at the Garden

Parks

- Parlee Beach Provincial Park

Nearby is Shediac, a lively town that caters to many visitors. A huge lobster statue, weighing 90 tonnes (99 tons), is displayed at Rotary Park — after all, this is the lobster capital of the world. During the annual Shediac Lobster Festival, parades, races, Acadian music, fireworks and lobster delicacies are on the menu. In summer, musicians entertain crowds at the Concert in the Park, Music at the Garden and Music Night on the Roof Top Patio. Just north of Shediac is Parlee Beach Provincial Park, boasting New Brunswick's favourite supervised swimming beach. Visitors may also indulge in ultimate frisbee, beach volleyball, picnicking and camping. The sand-sculpture contest is an annual event here.

Boardwalk on the sand dune.

8 BOUCTOUCHE

Museums and Historical Sites

- St. John the Baptist Church
- Musée de Kent (Kent Museum and Old Convent)

Arts and Culture

- Pays de la Sagouine

Parks

- Irving Eco-Centre: La Dune de Bouctouche (Sand Dune)

Further up the Acadian Coast is the small town of Bouctouche. Bouctouche is the birthplace of both the Acadian author Antonine Maillet and the industrialist K. C. Irving. Though he left here in 1925 for Saint John and later Bermuda, the late K. C. Irving's presence is still felt everywhere in Bouctouche: in the Irving Station and convenience store; in Kent Homes Ltd., the prefabricated-home factory; the white oil tanks; the donated carillon at St. John the Baptist Church; and the arboretum, chapel and main street that bear his name. He started out in this town with a small gas pump and a Ford car dealership, and by sheer determination built his own business empire. Although he and his family rose to become among the world's richest industrialists, the Irvings lived quietly in New Brunswick, largely unknown to the rest of Canada.

Also in town, we find the Irving Eco-Centre: La Dune de Bouctouche, a nature sanctuary par excellence. The Mi'kmaq

called this place "great little harbour," and the Acadians returning from exile in the late eighteenth century settled here. They saw Bouctouche's natural harbour as a future commercial port in their new Acadia. The sand dune, created within the harbour during the last ice age, was an important geographical feature to the fishing industry in that it served as shelter for fishers and their boats. In recent years, J. D. Irving Ltd. developed this dune as a shelter for wildlife and as an educational centre for the public, especially school children, to learn more about the dune, its ecology, shorebirds, mammals, plants and insects. The 2-kilometre (1.3-mile) boardwalk on the dune and through the salt marsh allows visitors to observe the dune's wildlife without disturbing the delicate surroundings. Adventurous types may want to walk the complete 12-kilometre (7.5-mile) length of the sand dune to the lighthouse, a five- to six-hour return trip.

ABOVE: Storytellers at Pays de la Sagouine.

RIGHT: A view of part of the site across the bridge.

The village of Bouctouche is also home to the Pays de la Sagouine, named after the fictional character and anti-hero created by the writer Antonine Maillet. The theme park Pays de la Sagouine is based on this fictional washerwoman, and the characters and houses on the site draw from the play. A wooden tower provides a view of the park, including a natural island and a long,

The chapel at Kent Museum and Old Convent.

winding boardwalk that leads to it. At the visitor centre, a short bilingual film presents the play's idea and an introduction to the Acadians. At times, Acadian music is performed and a rendition given in French of a monologue from the play. Short shows about Acadian lives are presented at different times per day in French and in English. Antonine Maillet wrote in 1984 that her birthplace was "balanced between two extremes: between a billionaire Irving and a Sagouine on her knees before her scrubbing pail; between the adventurers of the seas and the tillers of the earth; between the wealth of its traditions and its progressive ambitions; between its memory of the past and its dreams of the future."

Until 1964 the French village was also home of the Roman Catholic convent school for girls. The walls of the Kent Museum and Old Convent recall the days when the church took a keen interest in both the temporal and spiritual education of its youth — hence the convent. Life in the convent was strictly regulated for the seventy-five girls who lived here under the watchful eyes of Mother Superior: mass, breakfast, classes, lunch, afternoon classes, mass, garden work, then one hour of leisure time and to bed at nine. Most girls who graduated from the convent became teachers. In the 1960s the convent opened its school to local girls and boys, who would walk home after school. The Kent Museum shows the classroom, the nuns' quarters and the bedroom hall on the third floor. The small Gothic chapel (1879) on the second floor with its hand-sculptured altar, illusional ceiling beam painting and stenciled borders is very beautiful.

A view of the Richibucto River near Rexton.

9 REXTON

Museums and Historical Sites

- Bonar Law Common Historic Site

Arts and Culture

- Richibucto River Wine Estate
- Fromagerie au Fond des Bois

In Rexton, you cannot miss the tall, three-mast structure near the bridge honouring the early 1800s shipbuilders on the Richibucto River, predominantly the Jardine family. Here, on the bank of the Richibucto River in a beautiful park is also the Bonar Law Common Historic Site. This was the old boyhood home of Bonar Law, who became Britain's only prime minister born outside the United Kingdom. In 1850 his father, Reverend James Law, purchased the 9-hectare (22-acre) farm and established a Presbyterian manse. Today, costumed staff provide an interesting tour at the provincial site, which consists of the house supplied with late nineteenth-century furniture, barns with sheep, pigs and turkeys and farming implements. An interesting feature is the "beggar's bench" near the entrance. It opens into a bed and has a system to keep possible insects from getting out — a useful feature for unexpected guests. A more recent "ghostly" story at the house is the disappearance of Mrs. Law's purse that was laid out on the bed with her clothes — ask your guide about details! Once a week, you can attend a typical tea party at this historical site.

While in the area, you may want to take a vineyard tour and visit the only New Brunswick goat cheese farm. The Richibucto River Wine Estate in Mundleville on Route 495 is a scenic river location where you can get a tour of the vineyard producing the award-winning, cold-climate grape wines. Just a few minutes further down the street, the owner of the Fromagerie au Fond des Bois welcomes you with his horses and many friendly goats, who provide the milk for the cheese you are about to taste. Their assortment also includes cheese made from cow milk. Contact the farm and winery regarding their opening hours to avoid disappointments.

(10) KOUCHIBOUGUAC NATIONAL PARK

Parks

- Kellys Beach
- Major Kollock Creek Trail
- Osprey Trail
- The Bog Trail and Boardwalk

Established in 1969, the sizable Kouchibouguac National Park has 24,000 hectares (71,000 acres) and is the largest park in the province. The name Kouchibouguac derives from the Mi'kmaw language, meaning "river of the long tides." The park is basically flat land shaped by glaciers. Its major attractions are marine environments — salt marshes, the seashore, sand dunes, bogs and beaches. The water temperature in shallow lagoons may reach 20 degrees Celsius (68 degrees Fahrenheit) in July and August. Major activities are sunbathing, swimming and beachcombing at Kellys Beach, biking, canoeing and hiking. Bird watching is also excellent along the shore and on the marshes. There is a large network of gentle biking trails past wildflower fields, saltwater lagoons and Acadian woodland. Mountain bikers will enjoy the moderate 6.3-kilometre (3-mile) Major Kollock Creek Trail that leads through bogs, woodlands and sandy stretches. The park's 5-kilometre (3.2-mile) Osprey Trail at Loggieville invites hikers to view great blue herons, ospreys and terns along the beach section. Another attraction is the hanging red pine tree at the 2-kilometre (1.2-mile) LaSource River North walking trail. The Bog Trail's observation tower provides a good view across the ancient bog. A long boardwalk leads along pitcher plants, bakeapple, cotton grass and stunted black spruce to its end with a big red chair.

TOP: Kellys Beach.

ABOVE: A black bear sighting in the park!

6 NORTHEASTERN ACADIAN COAST

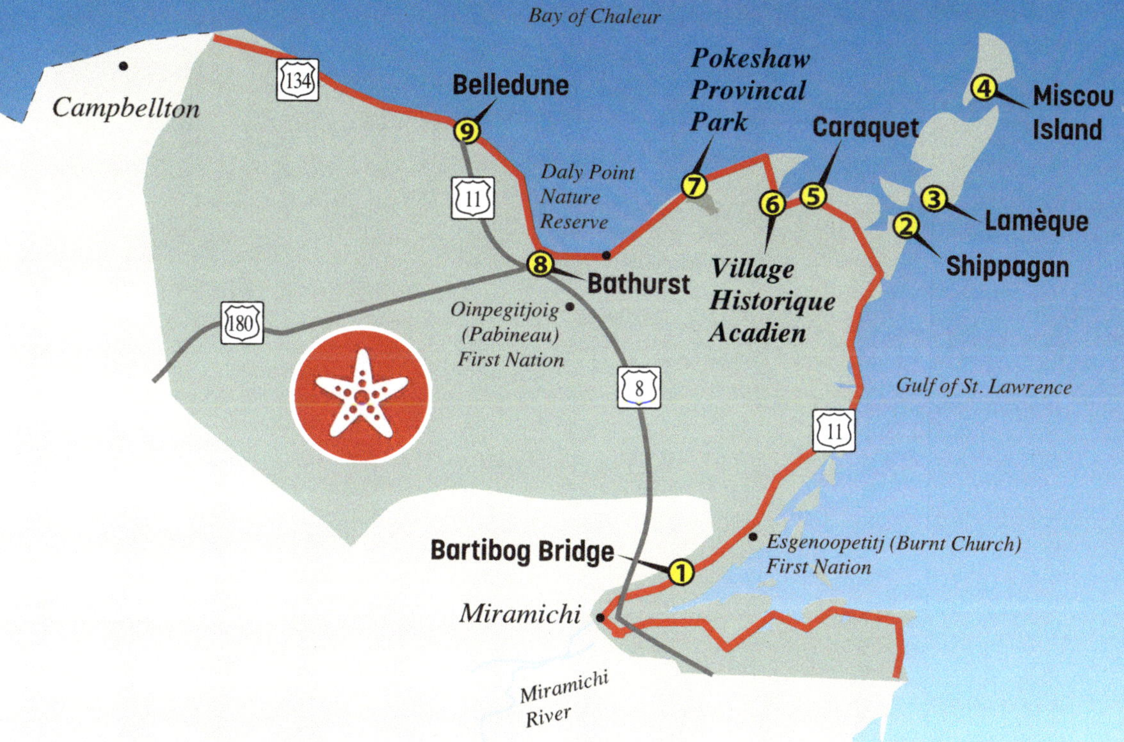

The northern section of the Acadian Coastal Drive skirts around the waters of Chaleur Bay (Baie de Chaleur) with its beaches, farms and fishing communities. This area is fiercely proud of its Acadian heritage: Acadian cuisine, Acadian fine art and music festivals, cultural festivals, the Village Historique Acadien and the Acadian flag. The choice of blue, white, red and yellow painted on mailboxes, lobster traps, garden chairs, barns and boats is not surprising, as these are the colours of the Acadian flag, which they flaunt in their towns and villages. In 1881, the starred French tricolour was adopted by the Acadians as their national flag. The yellow star represents Stella Maris (Star of the Sea) and the protection and guidance of the Blessed Virgin Mary. August 15, the Feast of the Assumption, has been National Acadian Day since 1881, and every year communities celebrate this anniversary with gusto. It underlines the importance of the Roman Catholic Church as the institution that took an interest in the lives of the Acadian people. The church established elementary schools and, in 1864, a French-language college in Memramcook near Moncton.

Horses pulling a carriage at MacDonad Farm.

1 BARTIBOG BRIDGE

Museums and Historical Sites

- MacDonald Farm historic site

North of the town of Miramichi, along Route 11, the Acadian Coastal Drive leads to the settlement of Bartibog Bridge. Nearby, the MacDonald Farm historic site at Miramichi Bay is a perfect backdrop for an 1820s family farm. Alexander MacDonald had served as a private soldier with the British forces in the American Revolutionary War and later as a justice of the peace, and the family was considered well off. The seven-room farmhouse, constructed with stones that came from Scotland as ballast, was home to Alexander MacDonald, his wife, Grace, and their thirteen children. The grounds, the wharf, the stone house and the view across the bay make this a choice spot. The ride on an old, red, horse-drawn wagon down to the farm offers a unique glimpse into the past. Jellies and jams from the olden days, still preserved by a thick layer of wax, line some kitchen shelves. A spice canister with a lock suggests how precious spices were in those days. Upstairs is an amazing seven-foot gun used for waterfowl hunting, requiring a steady hand indeed. And, of course, old MacDonald's farm has animals — among them horses, goats, pigs and chickens.

The many fishing boats in active harbours along the northeastern Acadian Coast show that fishing remains a powerful economic factor. Hundreds of fishers who live in coastal towns like Shippagan, Caraquet and Lamèque depend on lobster and snow crabs for a living. The "Acadian lobster" is exported worldwide and, according to local legend, the snow crab harvest, which began in the early 1970s, has created at least eighteen millionaires. In addition to fishing operations, there are prosperous peat moss operations and some blueberry farms. Fresh-off-the-boat seafood, warm sandy beaches, lighthouses, ecological parks, outdoor living museums and festivals and a first-class aquarium lure tourists to the area.

② SHIPPAGAN

Arts and Culture

- New Brunswick Aquarium and Marine Centre

ABOVE: Seals retrieving a ring at the New Brunswick Aquarium and Marine Centre.

INSET: The lighthouse next to the aquarium.

Northeast on Route 113, you reach the town of Shippagan and, beyond that, the charming twin islands of Lamèque and Miscou. Shippagan is considered the provincial capital of commercial fisheries. It is little surprise that the best seafood restaurants in all of New Brunswick are found in this area. Shippagan's leading attraction is the New Brunswick Aquarium and Marine Centre. This complex is devoted to the marine world and the fishing industry past and present. The hands-on display of a wheelhouse from a modern, high-tech fishing vessel is an interesting feature — a far cry from the wheels of olden days. The exhibits indicate the great variety of marine species — 125 of them — that inhabit the Gulf of St. Lawrence waters, including crabs, shrimps and urchins, as well as char, dogfish and red hake. The aquarium is home to a large variety of sea life, from the sturgeon with its spiny back to the rare blue lobster. Interactive displays enhance the visitor's experience. There is also an outdoor aquarium, where seals often stretch lazily in the sun. To see them in action, visit around feeding and show time at 11 a.m. and 4 p.m. They stay outside even in winter, when they are joined by three of their fellows from the Huntsman Marine Science Centre in St. Andrews.

At the Vet, Magical Sculpture Trail.

3 LAMÈQUE

Museums and Historical Sites

- Sainte-Cécile Church

Arts and Culture

- Provincial Peat Moss Festival
- International Baroque Music Festival
- Magical Sculpture Trail

Parks

- Ecological Park of the Acadian Peninsula (Lamèque Eco-Park)

North of Shippagan is Lamèque Island. During the annual Provincial Peat Moss Festival in July, the town of Lamèque honours the pioneers and workers of the peat moss industry. While you drive through the area, you may catch a glimpse of the harvest machines as they vacuum the peat moss off the thousands of years' old brown peat bogs. Peat moss harvesting is no cottage industry: Canada is the world's largest exporter of peat moss!

Also in July, Lamèque hosts the International Baroque Music Festival. For more than forty years this classical music festival has attracted people from near and far. The Sainte-Cécile Church, dedicated to the patron saint of musicians, has excellent acoustics. With its pastel-coloured interior of naïve art, it is a beautiful setting for the festival. Visitors will marvel at the vibrant colours of the folk-art decor of the church, also called the candy church! Nearby, in the village of Petite-Lamèque is the Magical Sculpture Trail with wood sculptures by Baromé Savoie. Here, we are greeted by a fox sticking his head under a fence. Be amused by the sow and her twelve sucklings, the Smurf family, and gaze at the story of the first settlers, carved skillfully into a tree trunk.

Around the corner at the Lamèque Eco-Park, we find an observation tower that overlooks a 0.5-kilometre (0.3-mile) interpretive boardwalk over a lagoon that leads to a small trail system through the Acadian forest. Bird watching is rewarding here.

The boardwalk on the Peat Bog Trail.

④ MISCOU ISLAND

Museums and Historical Sites

- Miscou Island Lighthouse National Historic Site

Parks

- Miscou Island Peat Bog Trail

Miscou Island is an important last stop for thousands of migratory birds, before they reach their southern wintering grounds. During migration, the shorebirds and waterfowl rest and feed along the island's beaches, in lagoons and peat bog ponds. Almost half of the island consists of peat bogs. The bogs are only fed by rainwater. One such area to explore is the Miscou Island Peat Bog Trail, an interpretative boardwalk loop with typical bog plants such as cotton grass, moss and the carnivorous sundews, pitcher plants and butterworts.

Continuing on the main road to its end is the Miscou Island Lighthouse National Historic Site of Canada. The lighthouse was built in 1856 to reduce the number of shipping accidents. The operational lighthouse still provides safe navigation for ships coming and going from the Gulf of St. Lawrence to Chaleur Bay. Today, you can visit this old and rare, octagonal, wooden, tapered building. Due to shore erosion, the lighthouse was moved 60 metres (197 feet) inland in 1945. A small park, beach and restaurant surround the lighthouse at the northeastern end of New Brunswick.

All dressed up for Tintamarre.

5 CARAQUET

Arts and Culture

- Le Festival Acadien de Caraquet

The town of Caraquet, founded in 1758, hosts a special week-long Acadian festival with concerts, the blessing of the fleet, Acadian food, plays and the Tintamarre (loud noise, din) parade on National Acadian Day. Tintamarre, the most colourful and unusual event of this festival, takes place on the Boulevard St. Pierre — Caraquet's main street — where a few blocks are closed to traffic. At 6 p.m. sharp, the Tintamarre madness begins. Residents dressed up in costumes walk along the main road back and forth from the junction with Rue de Cormier to the Old Convent. Participants make a great racket using pots, pans, whistles and cowbells, while visitors watch on the sidewalks and cheer them on. What is a pain to the ears is a feast for the eyes. Colourful costumes enliven the scene, but the red, white, blue and yellow of the Acadian flag dominates, whether it is worn as a dress or painted on a face. By about seven o'clock, the riotous parade is over.

The school, built in 1869, and the chapel, built in 1831.

6 VILLAGE HISTORIQUE ACADIEN

Museums and Historical Sites

- Mazerolle House
- Doucet House
- Babineau Farm

Arts and Culture

- Château Albert Hotel
- La Table des Ancêtres (the Ancestors' Table)
- Poirier Post House

A mere 10 kilometres (6.2 miles) west of Caraquet is one of the finest and most appealing of New Brunswick's heritage sites — the Village Historique Acadien. Maurice Basque, the scientific advisor of Acadian studies at the University of Moncton, describes it as "the best place to leap into the past and feel the atmosphere" and learn about daily life in Acadia in the nineteenth and early twentieth centuries. This award-winning living museum tells the story of the ingenuity and tenacity of the ancestors of the Acadian people after their expulsion in 1755.

The site is open from mid-June to mid-September. Allow three to four hours for a visit. This historic village is more than just a 2.2-kilometre (1.3-mile) walking tour with historical buildings; it also offers visitors an opportunity to see many old trades and crafts being practised throughout the village and to taste homemade Acadian meals.

There are women dyeing and spinning wool, weaving woollen goods and baking bread. The blacksmith shapes square-headed nails on his anvil. While one carpenter makes brooms, another shaves shingles and a cabinet-maker builds a perfect replica of a nineteenth-century chair.

ABOVE: Spinning in Robichaud House, built in 1846.

LEFT: The covered bridge, built in 1900.

The oldest house of about fifty original buildings in the village is the Martin House. Built in 1773, this humble trapper's cabin with a dirt floor once was home to seven people. Some houses have been transported to the site over long distances. The Mazerolle House, built in 1852, was brought here from Mazerolle Settlement, a former French community near Fredericton. Outside the house, the smell of fresh baking lingers as a costumed guide takes loaves out of a traditional outdoor oven.

At the Doucet House, a guide demonstrates the art of hand-dyeing wool. She uses all natural colours ranging from red to blue in a variety of earthen tones. Most of the colours are obtained by boiling roots or flowers like goldenrod, which produces a rich yellow. The guide uses one pound of flowers for every pound of dry wool she wants to dye. The blue was traditionally made by dissolving indigo in the urine of a twelve- or thirteen-year-old boy!

Working in the blacksmith shop, built in 1874.

The general store has beautiful glass panels imported from Belgium. There is also a tavern, and next to it the carpenter's shop, where broom making is the carpenter's specialty. He starts with the trunk of a young yellow birch, carefully shaving back thin strips of wood without cutting them off. He then folds all the strands back, ties them together and — voilà, there is a new broom! On the other side of the walkway another carpenter shows how shingles used to be made. Further on is the print shop showcasing *Le Moniteur Acadien*, the first Shediac newspaper from 1867. It took a week to produce, with singular letters lined up backwards in narrow columns and printed at the big Washington press, built in New York in 1860.

The blacksmith shop dates back to circa 1866. The blacksmith is usually busy making small implements or square-headed nails for horseshoes. He shapes the red-hot metal, dips it deep into a pail of water, and then offers the cooled product to visitors as souvenirs. At the far end of the village is the mill, also a pre-1900 vintage, which operates several times a day. From the back of the mill is a fine view of the one-room schoolhouse, the chapel and the mid-nineteenth-century Babineau Farm. Past these buildings are the cobbler's shop and the post house, from which a horse-drawn cart offers a ride around the village and back to the entrance.

The original Acadian village has expanded over the years, signifying life in the industrial era — 1890 to 1949. It now includes a shingle mill, a cooper's shop, a tinsmith's shop, a new farm complex, a covered bridge, a service station, a lobster hatchery and the Château Albert Hotel, a historical inn offering accommodations to travellers. The hotel was originally built in 1907 by Pierre P. Albert. During the First World War it served as headquarters for militia and training for the soldiers of the 165th Acadian Battalion, then became apartment rentals, a barrister's office, a drug store and general store until 1955 when it was destroyed by a fire. Beautifully restored and furnished to its original time, the visitor can experience old-fashioned charm here, not only by looking

TOP: The grist mill, built in 1895.

BOTTOM: An Irving Oil station, built in 1936.

at it, but by actually staying in the hotel.

Next to the hotel is the original Irving service station of 1936, transported from Sackville, New Brunswick. With the popularity of the automobile in the 1920s and 1930s came the necessity of service stations for gas and car repair, and K. C. Irving acted on this need. The company was looking for a special architecture for their service stations and came up with a turret designed by Sam Roy, which became the trademark for their stations throughout Canada.

During your visit to the village, you will certainly want to sit down for a drink or meal. Inside the historical village there are three restaurants. At the Dugas House is a small restaurant called La Table des Ancêtres (the Ancestors' Table), a great place to relax in a rustic atmosphere and enjoy homemade, hearty, Acadian food. In the Poirier Post House, you can get refreshments and simple meals for the whole family. You can also wine and dine at the Château Albert Hotel.

Pokeshaw Island in winter.

7 POKESHAW PROVINCIAL PARK

Near the Village Historique Acadien is a natural attraction that is equally unique. Pokeshaw Provincial Park overlooks two tiny islands, so-called flowerpot rocks or sea stacks that nature created over millennia by eroding soft sandstone until they became separated from the mainland. It is quite a sight to see the few remaining tree trunks, where cormorants like to congregate, and an Irish cross on top of the larger rock. The rock itself is white from bird excrement and fish leftovers. The park is open all year, allowing visitors to view the tidal waves pounding at the rock and sandy beach. Whatever the season, it is an impressive vista.

A winter day on the trails at Daly Point Nature Reserve.

8 BATHURST

Parks

- Daly Point Nature Reserve
- Tetagouche Nature Reserve and Falls
- Nepisiguit Mi'gmaq Trail
- Pabineau Falls

Another nature sanctuary is Daly Point Nature Reserve off Carron Drive in East Bathurst. The park of 33 hectares (100 acres) of salt marsh, coastline, fields and mixed forests was created by the Brunswick Mining and Smelting Corporation in 1989 to preserve the salt marsh habitat. A maze of beautiful trails skirts the area to an observation tower at Daly Point, overlooking the bay and the view towards Bathurst. Special attractions include Canada geese that arrive here on their migratory route in the fall. The unique value of this habitat is that the rare Maritime Ringlet butterfly thrives in the salt marsh. This is the only place in the world to find the Maritime ringlet butterfly!

The parking lot of the Daly Point Nature Reserve is also the trailhead of the 150-kilometre (93-mile) Nepisiguit Mi'gmaq Trail that leads from Bathurst all the way to the eastern end of Mount Carleton Provincial Park. A great idea for just an afternoon outing on this long-distance trek would be to drive to the access point "C - Red Brook" parking lot and hike the well-marked trail of moderate difficulty to the beautiful Pabineau Falls. In September and October, you may see Atlantic salmon jumping in the falls.

On the western side of Bathurst, about 10 kilometres (6 miles) along Highway 180, a short dirt road ends at a roundabout with a fenced-off lookout perched high above the beautiful Tetagouche Falls and gorge. Here at the Tetagouche Nature Reserve you also see remnants of a dam, built here in 1911–12 by businessman John P. Leger, who acquired the right to draw power from the Tetagouche Falls and financed his dream of a hydro-electric dam. This power-generating dam became the first of its kind in New Brunswick. Today, you can enjoy a picnic at the vista point and safely enjoy the scenery. You may want to hike down the short, steep trail to the bottom at the river and the pebbly beach for an amazing panoramic view and water access, but it may be difficult for some people.

TOP: The Nepisiguit River at Pabineau Falls.

BOTTOM: Tetagouche Falls.

9 BELLEDUNE 

Arts and Culture

- Devereaux blockhouse

Parks

- Jacquet River Gorge

Driving along Highway 11 from Bathurst, you'll find a spectacular vista point, the Jacquet River Gorge, off the beaten path. This gem is accessible by Archibald Road in Belledune. It is a protected natural area where you may see bears, moose, bald eagles, hawks, raccoons and other creatures in the gorge or on the wooded hills. The flaming colours of the Jacquet River Gorge are breathtaking in the fall. At the overlook, you may also meet the friendly Paul Devereaux. He welcomes visitors outside his colourful blockhouse and entertains and enlightens them with stories about the area, in which he has lived all his life.

ABOVE: A view over the Jacquet River Gorge.

INSET: Paul Devereaux.

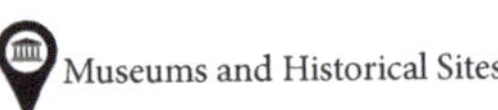
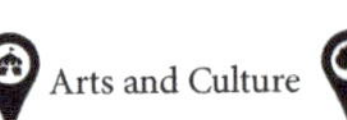

Museums and Historical Sites Arts and Culture Parks

7 MIRAMICHI RIVER VALLEY

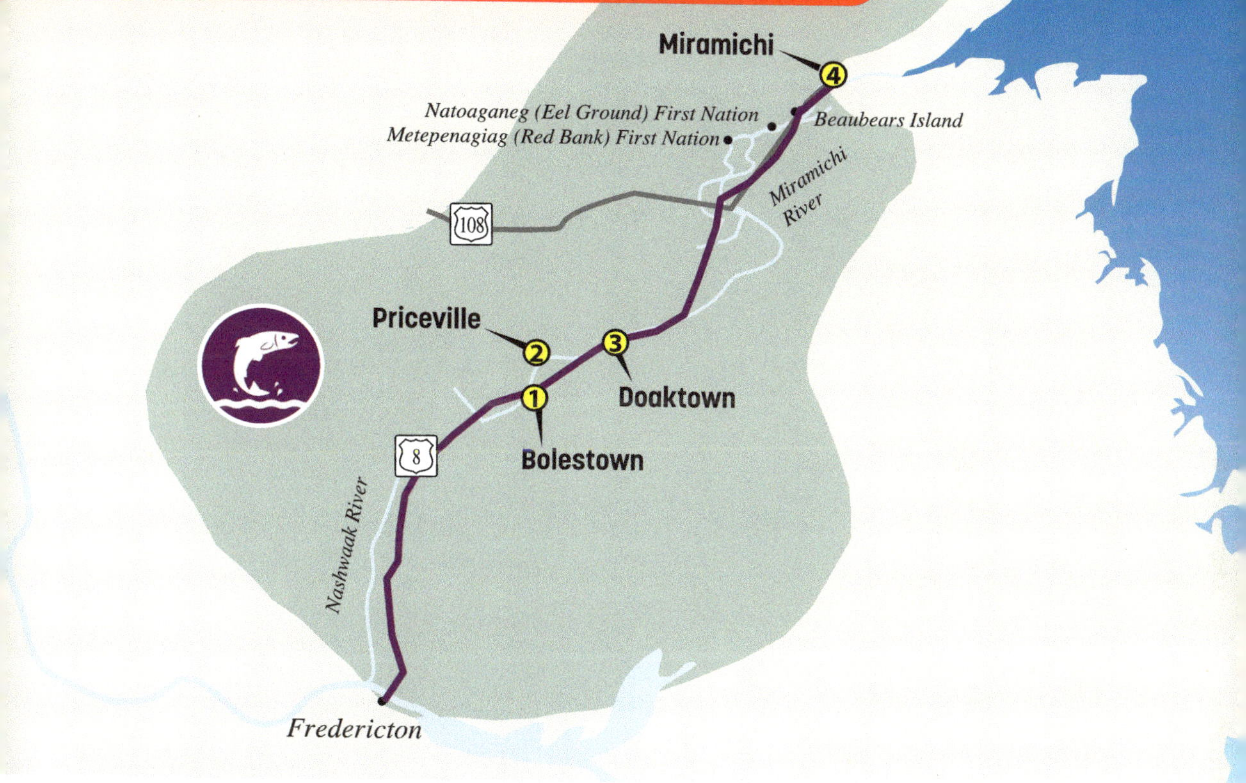

MIRAMICHI RIVER ROUTE

From the capital city of Fredericton to the city of Miramichi via Boiestown and Doaktown, the Miramichi River Route is a 173-kilometre (107-mile) drive through breathtaking wooded hills and salmon-fishing territory, first along the Nashwaak River and later, beyond Boiestown, the mighty Miramichi River. For over 3,000 years, the Atlantic salmon has been harvested in the Miramichi by the Mi'kmaq of Metepenagiag or Red Bank First Nation — New Brunswick's oldest village, which today pays tribute to Mi'kmaq ancestors in a heritage park that includes walking trails to archeological sites and an annual intertribal powwow. The great stands of pine forests at the river's edge attracted British, Irish and Scots to the area as entrepreneurs and lumbermen in the early nineteenth century. The river drives of logs to the mills during the spring freshets are no more, but wood harvesting and pulp and sawmill operations are still economically important for the region.

① BOIESTOWN 

Museums and Historical Sites

- Central New Brunswick Woodmen's Museum

The Central New Brunswick Woodmen's Museum in Boiestown pays tribute to the lumbering history of the area in the early 1800s, when Thomas Boies from New Hampshire started a lumber mill there. This outdoor museum comprises over twenty original buildings, a train and hundreds of tools, The main building has a life-like exhibit of animals mounted about 100 years ago by a local taxidermist.

ABOVE: "Old" loggers' houses at the Central New Brunswick Woodmen's Museum.

INSET: The former rail station at the Woodmen's Museum.

The 200-metre McNamee-Priceville Footbridge.

2 PRICEVILLE

Parks

- McNamee-Priceville Footbridge

Following the River Route 8 north into Priceville and towards the Miramichi River's shore is New Brunswick's longest suspension bridge. In 1938, three people at a time were allowed to cross the 204-metre (630-foot) footbridge to McNamee. Today, a plaque reminds us of the tragic bridge accident in mid-May 1939 during the spring freshet. While five people crossed over during high water, a cold, wild current swept over the bridge, taking three men to their deaths. Among them was Tennyson Price, who was crossing to McNamee to pick up his marriage license. Two subsequent footbridges were built, both with a middle abutment, making them swing way over the expected high-water currents in the spring.

The area's excellent angling was kept a secret by Miramichi residents, but by the 1920s, after the pulp mill industry was firmly established, the locals found a lucrative sideline — guiding sport fishers eager to experience the thrill of reeling in an Atlantic salmon weighing 9–13 kilograms (20–30 pounds), one of the best fighting fish anywhere. Up along the several branches of the Miramichi, the rich and often famous made their annual pilgrimages to "the camp," i.e., well-appointed fishing lodges located near salmon pools. Over the years, small towns like Blackville and Doaktown developed facilities to serve the needs of sport fishers. With declining fish numbers, strict fishing quotas and a hook-and-release policy were imposed to save the salmon. Commercial salmon fishing in New Brunswick was banned to ensure the salmon's survival. The Atlantic salmon's life cycle comprises six stages: egg, alevin, fry, parr, smolt and adult. Born in a freshwater river, the salmon live their whole life in the ocean before returning to the river of their birthplace six years later as adults for spawning. After starving, they will die in the same river they were born in.

TOP: Bloomers on the line at Doak Provincial Heritage Site.

LEFT: A re-enactor spinning wool.

3 DOAKTOWN

Museums and Historical Sites

- Atlantic Salmon Museum
- Doak Provincial Heritage Site

The Atlantic Salmon Museum in Doaktown pays tribute to the king of game fish as a source of food and trade in past and present. It displays a large array of tackle; poaching gear, including illegal spears; drift netting gear; jig hooks; and even dynamite.

Up the street from the Atlantic Salmon Museum is the Doak Provincial Heritage Site, a living museum commemorating the Doak family, who in the early 1800s arrived from Scotland at this trade post between Newcastle (now Miramichi) and Fredericton during a terrible storm. Originally, they had planned to continue on to Kentucky, but decided to settle in this area of abundant forests and salmon. The Doak family bought the devaluated Betts farm and soon developed it into a respectable homestead. Robert "Squire" Doak became one of the leading entrepreneurs of the region in the 1800s. At the entrance, a guide in period costume takes visitors across the fields to the Doak House, constructed in 1822. Robert Doak's career reads like this: 1822, overseer of the poor; 1823, supervisor in charge of highways; 1825, justice of the peace; 1826, school trustee; 1829, acting coroner.

The furniture in the Doak House is original and not collected from various buildings as at other heritage sites in New Brunswick. The living room features a piano organ and a gramophone, items that indicate the wealth of the inhabitants. The adjacent room and the sewing room, with its solid wood window shutters, were Mrs. Doak's domain. Upstairs is the boys' room and a room for a live-in minister! The latter room has painted floors, another sign of wealth, and a bed painted green and pink. Other features of the site today are the community vegetable garden, a large barn used as a seasonal produce market and the Woolly Croft with weaving and carding demonstrations.

Ritchie Wharf Park.

4 MIRAMICHI

Museums and Historical Sites

- Wilson's Point historic site
- Beaubears Island

Arts and Culture

- Ritchie Wharf Park
- Beaverbrook childhood home
- Miramichi Folksong Festival
- Miramichi Irish Festival

Parks

- French Fort Cove Park

The city of Miramichi is picturesquely located at the mouth of Miramichi Bay, where the mighty Miramichi River meets the salty waters of the Northumberland Strait. Miramichi City, which comprises Newcastle, Chatham and Douglastown, is spread out on both sides of the river. Walking trails and French Fort Cove Park invite the public to enjoy the waterfront by foot, canoe or kayak. The newly erected Ritchie Wharf Park is a nautical theme park with docking facilities, restaurants, a playground and a picnic area. A taste of the river's cuisine is a must when in town. Local specialties are grilled salmon, pheasant stew and fiddleheads picked from the river banks.

Miramichi's most famous son is Sir Max Aitken (1879–1964), who became a financier in Canada, a politician and newspaper baron in London and a benefactor. He was made a lord and took the title "Beaverbrook" from a Miramichi hamlet he knew as a child. His stately boyhood home on King George Highway in Miramichi-Newcastle, the old Presbyterian manse, is not far from

The Centennial Bridge over the Miramichi River.

the town square, where a bust stands in his memory. In the 1940s, Lord Beaverbrook became intensely interested in his roots and, though he remained an influential figure in London's political and financial world for the rest of his life, he made long summer visits to his beloved Miramichi. He asked the local librarian, Louise Manny, to collect some of the old lumbermen's songs he had heard as a boy. Manny asked the public for help, and the public responded with great enthusiasm. She recorded the traditional woodsmen's and farmers' songs and presented her growing collection in a Sunday radio show.

In 1958, Louise Manny organized the first Miramichi Folksong Festival. This summer event is the longest-running festival in Canada. It offers a variety of styles, from fiddle tunes such as "Don Messer's Break Down" and "Turkey in the Straw" to Irish, Scottish and modern dances, from medleys of war songs to gospel music.

Miramichi is also home to Canada's first and largest Irish Festival. The festival celebrates the contribution made by the early settlers and their descendants. The Irish began coming to the Maritimes in large numbers in 1847 in search of a better life. The potato famine in Ireland was at its worst in 1848 and 1849, and without sufficient aid from the mainland, the Irish had little choice but to flee in ever greater numbers. At least one million had left Ireland by 1851.

The annual walking parade in Miramichi

sets the tone for the Irish Festival, with players of Celtic pipes and drums, Irish dancers and hundreds of descendants from the early Irish settlers bearing the names Kelly, Fitzpatrick, O'Toole and Ronan. The parade travels from James M. Hill Memorial High School to Lord Beaverbrook Arena, which is fittingly decorated in Protestant orange and Catholic green, with a neutral white separating the two. The festival offers an ambitious program of singers, dancers, fiddlers, pipers and drummers. Irish children perform traditional figure dancing, reels and slip jig dancing and the Celtic River dance.

Two important heritage sites in Miramichi are Wilson's Point historic site and Beaubears Island. Located across from each other where the northwest Miramichi and the southwest Miramichi converge, the sites are easy to reach by boat — it's a much

ABOVE: Dancers at the Miramichi Irish Festival.

BELOW: Catching the ferry to Beaubears Island.

The interpretive centre at Wilson's Point historic site.

longer stretch from one to the other by car.

Beaubears Island is named after Lieutenant Boishébert, a corruption of the French name. The island was a hunting and fishing ground for the Mi'kmaq, and early French settlers arrived in the mid-1600s. Nicolas Denys was a French pioneer who established French trading posts across from the island in Miramichi-Nelson. Beaubears Island and Wilson's Point are known for being the site of the Acadian refugee Camp d'Espérance (Camp of Hope). Led by Lieutenant Boishébert in anticipation of a strategic point for New France to defend this area, hundreds of Acadians fled to the island in 1756 to escape deportation ordered by British rulers. In the harsh winter of 1756–57, hundreds of Acadian refugees died there of famine and smallpox, one of the most horrible events of the Acadian deportation. Today, a boat ride from the interpretive centre to Beaubears Island allows visitors to walk on the undisturbed archeological grounds of the Mi'kmaq encampments, the Acadian refugee camp, and a New Brunswick shipbuilding enterprise from the nineteenth century.

Wilson's Point at the Enclosure Road in Derby Junction just outside of Miramichi proper also marks a significant place where early Scottish settlers, such as William Davidson, landed in the 1760s, merely ten years after Boishébert's soldiers were staying here to defend New France. You can walk on the grounds amidst large pine trees to an ancient graveyard, a wharf and a replica of the little "kirk" (church) of 1791, built without any nails!

8 APPALACHIAN RANGE

APPALACHIAN RANGE ROUTE

The Appalachian Range Route is a 224-kilometre (140-mile) drive from Perth-Andover to Campbellton through North America's oldest mountains, the Appalachians. The route first follows the Tobique River to Plaster Rock, the southern gateway to Mount Carleton Provincial Park, featuring the highest summit in the Maritimes. The route then leads through Saint-Quentin, the western gateway to the provincial park, and a lively French community. The drive winds through the Restigouche uplands to Kedgwick and from there to Campbellton at Chaleur Bay. The rivers and lakes in the uplands were used as canoe routes by early inhabitants.

The logging industry also used the waterways to float timber to nearby sawmills. The Upper Restigouche River, now a Canadian heritage river, offers great opportunities for recreation, such as fishing the famed, large Atlantic salmon. About 15,000 to 25,000 active salmon enter the Restigouche River each year, and people from all over the globe come to the Restigouche River Lodge to get the chance to catch one. Canoeing day trips with historical and nature interpretation, bald eagle and Atlantic salmon sightings, Fall Brook Falls, picnics and swimming are offered on the Restigouche by various companies. The entire Saint-Quentin/ Kedgwick area boasts a flourishing maple sugar industry and enjoys a reputation as the maple syrup capital of New Brunswick. In mid-March and early April, you may want to visit a sugaring-off operation, learn about the maple sap production and taste taffy on the snow.

① CAMPBELLTON

Museums and Historical Sites

- Miguasha (UNESCO fossil site across the bridge in Quebec)

Arts and Culture

- Salmon Festival
- Sugarloaf Mountain Provincial Park
- Sugarloaf Mountain Bike Park

Parks

- Waterfront Esplanade
- Sugarloaf Provincial Park and Summit Trail

Highway 17 heads north to Campbellton through the forested hills of the Appalachian mountain range, where lumbering was and still is a mainstay of the economy. Campbellton is located in the Appalachian Mountains on one side and at the mouth of the powerful Restigouche River on the other. It was off this coast that the last naval battle for the possession of Canada was fought in 1760. There is a plaque at the Waterfront Esplanade remembering this last naval engagement of the Seven Years' War (1756–63) between a French frigate and a superior British force. The French commander scuttled two of his ships in the shallow waters of the Restigouche Estuary after being trapped here, so that the British would not capture them. This accelerated the fall of New France. The Waterfront Esplanade is a beautiful park on the south bank of the Restigouche River that allows scenic views of the majestic interprovincial J. C. Van Horne Bridge and the mountains across on the Gaspé Peninsula in Quebec. You can take in the scenery and stroll along the Restigouche River, gaze at sculptures like the impressive 8.5-metre (28-foot) sculpture of the Atlantic salmon, nicknamed "Restigouche Sam," enjoy the waterfalls, have a picnic, climb onto an oversized, red bench or swing on a red rocking bench.

J. C. Van Horne Bridge crossing to Quebec.

ABOVE: View from Sugarloaf Mountain onto Campbellton.

INSET: Sugarloaf Mountain rising in the distance.

On the other side of the town, Campbellton's Sugarloaf Mountain dominates the scenery. Viewed from Campbellton, a two-peaked mountain appears, just like the famous Sugarloaf in Rio. Viewed from the Acadian Coastal Drive coming from Bathurst, Sugarloaf appears as a one-peaked natural phenomenon.

Campbellton really comes to life in early summer during its annual Salmon Festival, when the town celebrates the prized sport fish with delicious treats and tournaments. Year-round recreational possibilities such as jogging, hiking, biking and alpine skiing make the city's Sugarloaf Provincial Park a popular destination. Hiking the 5-kilometre (3-mile) distance up and down the Sugarloaf Summit Trail is quite a workout, but the reward is a breathtaking view across Campbellton, Chaleur Bay and the Gaspé Peninsula with its UNESCO fossil site Miguasha, a thirty-minute drive from Campbellton into Quebec. The Sugarloaf summit provides one of the finest views in New Brunswick. During the summer, you can stay at the wooded campground. The park also offers nice cabins and cute yurts.

Next to the actual Sugarloaf Mountain, the site features a unique downhill bike park that offers a lift service for mountain bikers. The trails are jam-packed with berms, table tops, drops, step-ups and other wooden features. There are trails for beginners and experienced bikers.

② SAINT-QUENTIN

Arts and Culture

- Western Festival
- Maple Festival

A 40-kilometre (25-mile) drive from Mount Carleton Provincial Park is Saint-Quentin, a service town to the park and host to the biggest Western Festival in the Maritimes. Events include the usual bronco riding, bull riding, barrel racing, calf roping and steer wrestling, as well as music and dance. The town also organizes an annual winter carnival and, as the maple capital of Atlantic Canada, a Maple Festival in early spring.

Bronco riding and fire breathing at the Western Festival.

A view of Nictau Lake from Mount Sagamook.

③ MOUNT CARLETON

Parks

- Nictau Lake
- Nepisiguit Lake
- Mount Sagamook Trail

Mount Carleton Provincial Park was created in 1969 as a step to preserve a pocket of wilderness in New Brunswick. It is by far the largest provincial park in New Brunswick and boasts Mount Carleton, the highest elevation in the Maritimes, standing 820 metres (2,693 feet) tall. Since altitude affects climate, lower temperatures near the peaks are to be expected at any time of the year, along with snow from mid-October to mid-May. Moose, black bears, and deer all live here, even though hunting pressure outside the park has been severe for many years. This is the country of Charles G. D. Roberts's *The King of Mamozekel*, a coming-of-age story of a young moose and its encounters with porcupines, lynxes, bears, fellow moose, and hunters.

In the early 1900s, when big game and salmon were abundant, the area attracted hunters and fishers from outside the province, particularly from Connecticut. They set up fishing and game camps along the Nictau and Nepisiguit Lakes, and sometimes even created trails. The remarkable Mount Sagamook Trail still follows an old path established in the early 1900s by Admiral Spruance, an avid sportsman from Connecticut. A spectacular view from the peak of Mount Sagamook of Nictau Lake and the adjacent mountains makes this strenuous hike worthwhile. The park has a total of 62 kilometres (39 miles) of hiking and backpacking trails offering scenic views, waterfalls, lakes, summits, rocky ridges, forests and a restored fire tower. Other activities are camping, bird watching, biking, boating and swimming as well as cross-country skiing in winter.

ACKNOWLEDGEMENTS

We are thankful to the many people at the historical and natural sites, outdoor museums and festivals for taking the time to explain the history and heritage behind the obvious. Special thanks are due to Leslie Lewington of the Doak Provincial Heritage Site for a great tour we got even beyond the official closing time. Debbie Hickey of Hampton's Kings County Museum had many stories about the old jail and scary-looking dolls. We are grateful to Jennifer Stead at the Florenceville art gallery for her detailed information about the local art scene and the sculptures, buildings and events in town. We also thank the knowledgeable and passionate guides we do not know by name, but whose in-depth explanations were way beyond what you'd expect on a regular tour. They include the costumed guides at the beautiful Kings Landing and at the Bonar Law historic site in Rexton. The guide at the Keillor House in Dorchester, at the Steeves House in Hillsborough, Le Pays de Sagouine in St. Antoine, the Sheriff Andrews House in St. Andrews, the Roosevelt Cottage and F.U.N. tour on Campobello Island, the Connell House in Woodstock, the 8th Hussars in Sussex, the Place des Pionniers in the New Brunswick Panhandle and at the NB Military History Museum in Gagetown. Last, but certainly not least, we'd like to express our gratitude to Jim Lorimer, Sarah Mack and Katie Button of Formac Publishing for their assistance and encouragement.

— Marianne and H. A. Eiselt

INDEX